THE ULTIMATE BRAIN HEALTH
PUZZLE BOOK FOR ADULTS

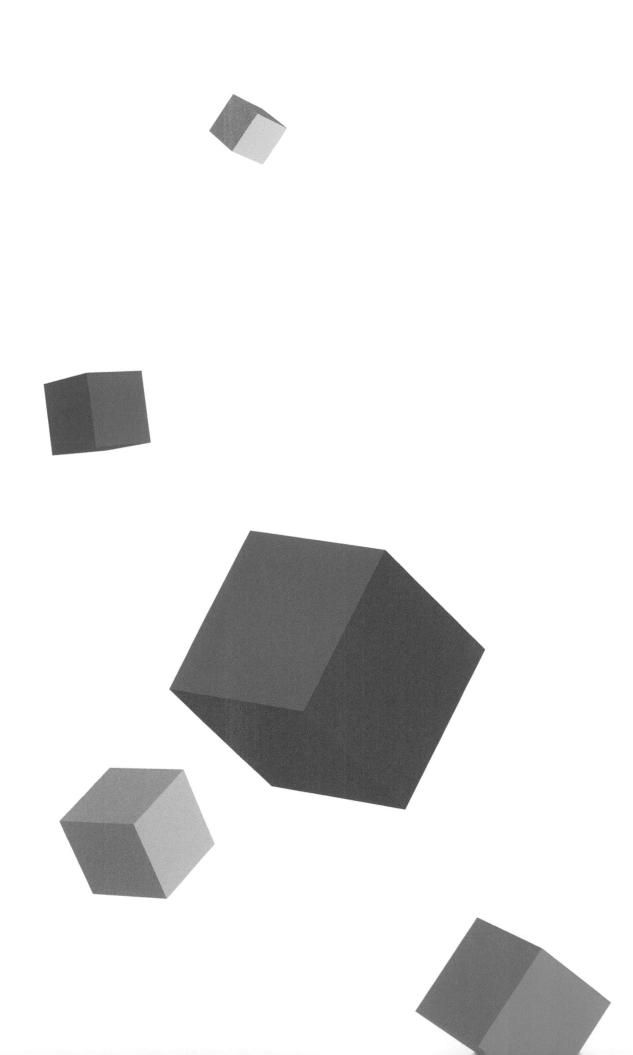

THE ULTIMATE
BRAIN
HEALTH
PUZZLE
BOOK
FOR ADULTS

Crosswords, Sudoku, Cryptograms, Word Searches, and More!

Phil Fraas

ROCKRIDGE
PRESS

Interior and Cover Designer: Darren Samuel
Editor: Mary Colgan
Art Producer: Meg Baggott
Production Editor: Ashley Polikoff

ISBN: 978-1-64611-408-5

R3

CONTENTS

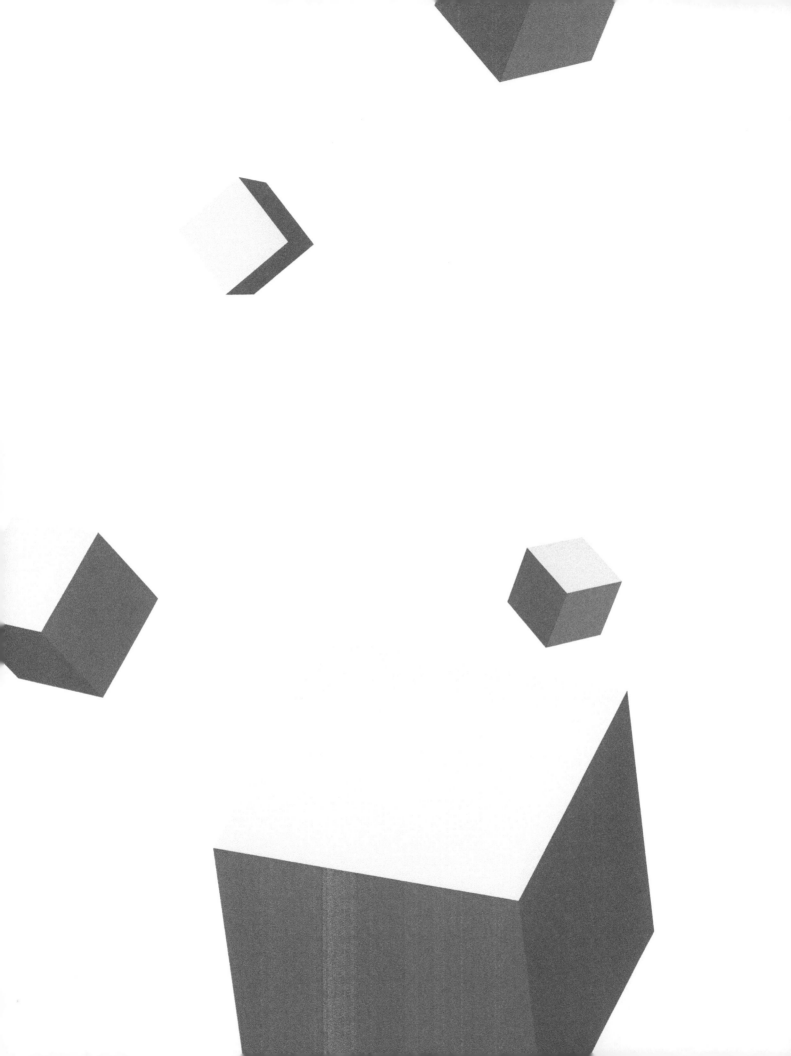

INTRODUCTION

Many adults are realizing that keeping their brains healthy is as important as taking care of their bodies. While we exercise and maintain a nutritious diet for our physical well-being, what steps do we take to optimize brain health? What are the mental equivalents of aerobics, weight training, and avoiding unhealthy foods? No one has the definitive answers, but there seems to be universal agreement that working puzzles can benefit the brain, even in small ways. Anything that helps strengthen cognitive functioning and stave off degeneration of the brain as we age is a step in the right direction.

Puzzle challenges make us use our brain differently than we do in our day-to-day life. When we take on a puzzle, we stretch beyond our routine. And puzzle challenges use many of our brain's facilities, including observational and deductive skills, short-term memory, and creative imagination. No wonder our brains like them—puzzles are a good workout for the old noodle.

So, this book is designed to help you strengthen your thinking skills. We provide a wide array of puzzles, each requiring a different brain skill. We want you to use as many mental "muscles" as possible. The book includes crosswords, cryptograms, word searches, calcudoku, sudoku, and logic puzzles.

Plus, if you like puzzles at all (and almost everyone does), I would like to tell you something that is more fun than simply giving them a go, working on them, and then reaching for the answer key. More fun than that is solving them! Prevailing over the evil machinations of the dastardly puzzle constructor trying to frustrate you is very enjoyable, even rewarding.

The way this book is set up allows you to find your balance. We don't throw you into the deep end right away. We realize it takes a little practice and trial and error to build up the ability to work a particular type of puzzle, and do it well. So, chapter 1 gives you a sampling of each of the six types of puzzles to use as a warm-up. For each type of puzzle, I also share my opinion about its brain health benefits, and I offer suggestions on how to approach solving it. In chapter 2, there are more puzzles at an easy level, and in chapter 3, the difficulty is dialed up a notch to the medium level. Finally, chapter 4 offers puzzles we consider the most challenging, and require the most mental effort to solve. This book's progressive structure enables you to hone your skills and develop solving techniques before you dive into the deep end.

All puzzles in this book were constructed with you in mind. As I worked putting the puzzles together, I continually asked myself: How do I make these puzzles fun as well as challenging? My goal is to offer puzzles so enjoyable you will want to work and progress from one level to the next all the way through to the end of the book. It is said "the proof of the pudding is in the eating," and I hope that as you work your way through the puzzles in this book, you find it is a pleasant repast!

WARM-UP

GETTING STARTED WITH CROSSWORDS

Brain Health Benefits

Working crosswords requires the use of your memory, vocabulary, and creative thinking. Although part of solving crosswords is drawing on words you use frequently, you must also winkle out words that are in the back of your mind rather than on the tip of your tongue. As you progress through the puzzle, filled-in letters will offer hints that lead to solving clues that had you stumped only a moment before, which keeps your mind active and engaged and gives you the satisfaction of multiple victories within one puzzle. And the more puzzles you do, the more these results are compounded! More crosswords means more opportunities for adding words to your vocabulary, improving your spelling skills, and keeping your reasoning skills sharp.

How to Solve

Solve the clues to fill in the puzzle grid. A little tip if you're new to crosswords: Don't feel the need to start at the top left corner and follow the clues in order. Skip around and see what words you can fill in right away to give you a head start on the others.

You can create "footholds" in the puzzle grid by filling in likely suffixes, such as -s when the clue indicates the answer is plural, -ed when it's a past-tense verb, and so on. Also, be alert for clues within clues. The clue "gold, in Guadalajara" tells you that the clue is asking for the Spanish word for "gold." If the clue contains an abbreviation, like "cooking meas.," that means the answer is an abbreviation, too.

Finally, if you run into a clue that seems obscure or asks for vocabulary you're not familiar with, work your way around it. You might fill in the word just by solving crossing words. Crossword creators sometimes use unfamiliar words as bridges to make the rest of the puzzle work. Plus, when you get to the solution, you'll have added a new word to your vocabulary!

SEEING RED

DID YOU KNOW?

A healthy diet with fruits and vegetables can slow aging in the brain.
Invite berries, leafy greens, and dark chocolate to dinner.
Eating healthy improves blood flow to the brain, and the brain loves it.

Across

1. Clemson athlete
6. Fill a suitcase
10. ____ *Good Men* (1992 flick in which Cruise and Nicholson do battle)
14. *Gladiator* setting
15. Natural balm
16. Cork's country
17. Sweet treat
19. Mardi ___
20. "Trick" joint
21. They come before xi in the Greek alphabet
22. Catholic clergyman
24. Facts and figures
26. Barnyard honker
27. Tree juice
30. Learn, discover
32. 40 winks
35. Harasses (someone) online
37. Embroil
39. French farewell
40. Scott Joplin's "Maple Leaf ___"
41. Labors, slaves away
42. Do for some hipsters
44. Car's hood, to the English
45. Store posting: Abbr.
46. Harness racer
48. Nunnery has three
49. Three-time Wimbledon champ
51. "If all ___ fails . . . "
53. Stop working, for good
55. Lennon's mate
56. Swerve
60. Chows down
61. Fruit of the Fragaria × ananassa
64. Largest of seven
65. Subsequently
66. Come up
67. Meadows
68. Chimney coating
69. Units of force, in physics

Down

1. Bulletin board fastener
2. Persia, today
3. DNA unit
4. _____ on a high note (finished with a success)
5. Romano or Liotta
6. Resident of Port Moresby
7. Swiss peaks
8. Rank above major: Abbr.
9. Block access to (with "of")
10. Auspices, patronage
11. Big piece of emergency equipment
12. "Big band" and "Victorian," for two
13. On a map, it is to the left
18. Those opposed
23. Muscles that control some arm and leg movements
25. Nervously excited
26. Big cousin of a cymbal
27. Kind of infection
28. Passion
29. Small decorative plant that is seasonally popular
31. Passed around, as cards
33. Woody or Tim _____
34. Annoyances
36. Early rocket expert Willy ___
38. Oui's opposite
40. Donnybrook
43. Collars, takes in
44. Not on deck
47. Lessee
50. Travel documents
52. Antonym for none
53. Word before estate or number
54. Alleviate
55. Black-and-white cookie
57. She replaced Pam at the front desk on *The Office*
58. Gaelic tongue
59. Deli breads
62. Even if, briefly
63. Michael Jackson album

ANSWER ON PAGE 125

GETTING STARTED WITH CRYPTOGRAMS

Brain Health Benefits

Cryptograms can strengthen your reasoning skills. These puzzles require a disciplined use of trial and error, a methodology for solving problems. You start by formulating a theory, e.g., a certain three-letter coded word is "the," and then test it out. If it leads to a dead end, you adjust your attack accordingly. More so than crosswords, cryptograms rely on creative imagination. With crosswords, intersecting words can help you figure out an answer, but cryptograms do not afford you that luxury.

How to Solve

We have taken an interesting quote from a person of note and converted all the letters in both the quote and the person's name into a straightforward code. Each letter is represented by a different letter. Your challenge is to "decode" all the letters in the cryptogram to reveal the quote and name of the person who said it.

To get started, look for single-letter words that are most likely "a" or "I", as well as other common words such as "the", which happens to contain three of the most commonly used letters in the alphabet. You can also look for clues such as apostrophes that indicate possessives or contractions. Also, the title of the cryptogram contains a hint. For instance, if the quote is about fathers, there's a fair chance that a three-letter combination could stand for "dad." Finally, if you get stuck, you can find a hint for each puzzle on page 124. Happy solving!

PLEASANT TIMES

IRVVYP QGMYPJWWJ—IRVVYP QGMYPJWWJ; MW

VY MDWIY DQEY QAUQHI KYYJ MDY MUW VWIM

KYQRMTGRA UWPNI TJ MDY YJXATID AQJXRQXY.

—DYJPH LQVYI

HINTS (SEE PAGE 124): 7, 28, 30
ANSWER ON PAGE 125

GETTING STARTED WITH WORD SEARCHES

Brain Health Benefits

Word searches can strengthen focus and visual-spatial skills. It takes persistence to scour the grid for embedded words. To recognize letters grouped in ways that indicate the possibility of a word, you must look in different directions, including horizontally (left to right, and vice versa), vertically (down or up), or diagonally. While straightforward word searches use familiar positioning (with the string of letters set in a straight line), all word searches, like the ones in this book, require you to hold and manipulate images in your mind—more good exercise for the brain.

How to Solve

Words may be hidden vertically, horizontally, or diagonally, and both forward and backward. A good way to get started is to look for a word with a less common letter—like a Q—which will be easier to spot. Keep in mind that that grid will be stuffed with as many words as possible. Perhaps 80 percent of the letters will be part of a word you are searching for. So, more often than not, whatever letter you happen to look at will lead you to a hidden word spelled out in one of eight directions.

 **PUZZLE ON NEXT PAGE**

GEORGE WASHINGTON

```
N X Y M R A Z A I N I G R I V
A F V C F V P L T F I R S T H
M V A S U A N A A W Q R C O Y
S I R R T L L O C R E H N E U
E C I R M L V S N P E O C L M
T T I K N E U K E R R N I W E
A O P O T Y R W R T E B E U C
T R S R T F I Y A D E V F G I
S A U I A O T Q N R E E T O V
M S N T I R K E T U H G T M R
T U H D E G P Y R Y L E C H E
V E U E J E A T W O T E R M S
R T N E D I S E R P O T A O S
Y R E N V I K A H T R A M D C
T C I V I C X O Y T I N G I D
```

ARMY	FIRST	MT. VERNON	TWO TERMS
CHERRY TREE	GENERAL	PATRIOT	UNITY
CIVIC	HONOR	PRESIDENT	VALLEY FORGE
DIGNITY	INDEPENDENCE	SERVICE	VICTOR
DUTY	LEAD	STATESMAN	VIRGINIA
FALSE TEETH	LIBERTY	TALL	WAR HERO
FARMER	MARTHA	TRUE	
FATHER	MASON	TRUST	ANSWER ON PAGE 125

GETTING STARTED WITH CALCUDOKU

Brain Health Benefits

Working on calcudoku puzzles can strengthen your deductive reasoning skills, creative thinking, and short-term memory because it requires you to use all three throughout the activity. A player approaches a calcudoku puzzle by using creative thinking to develop possible solutions and testing them. Testing your hypotheses gives your short-term memory a workout. Being able to play one, two, and three moves ahead is how you play this game and solve a calcudoku puzzle.

How to Solve

To solve the calcudoku puzzle, fill each empty cell in the grid with a number 1 through 4 (or 5, 6, or 7, depending on the size of the grid) so that each row (across) and column (down) contains all of the numbers, with no repeats. The cells of the grid are arranged in "cages" of two or more cells. Each cage has a small number and arithmetic symbol in the upper-left corner as a clue to which numbers belong there. For example, a clue of 3+ in a two-celled cage means that the two numbers added together should equal 3. Single-cell cages simply designate the number that belongs there.

In cages with three or more cells that require subtraction or division (symbolized by ":"), you perform the calculation for each of the smaller possible numbers against the largest number. For example, if the clue for a three-cell cage is "1:" and you deduce that 6, 3, and 2 would fit in the cage, you would test your answer like so: 6:3 = 2; 2:2 = 1. Voilà!

To get started, first fill in any single-cell cage and look for cages for which there can be only one answer, such as a three-cell cage in a straight line that gives the clue 6+, since the only possible numbers can be 1, 2, and 3.

CALCUDOKU 1

ANSWER ON PAGE 125

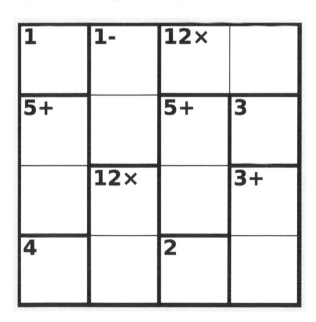

GETTING STARTED WITH SUDOKU

Brain Health Benefits

Working on sudoku puzzles can strengthen your deductive reasoning and attention to detail. Prefilled numbers are valuable clues for you to determine whether there is only one possible number to fill a cell. To make this determination, you must employ a systematic analytical approach, which is a good deductive reasoning exercise. It is also important to focus on details. Many times (to my chagrin), I have found myself in a blind alley. How did I get there? Usually, I failed to recognize a number embedded in a clump of other numbers when I surveyed the sudoku grid.

How to Solve

To solve a 9x9 sudoku puzzle, fill in each cell with a number from 1 to 9 so that each row, column, and 3x3 "cage" contains each number, with no repeats. There can be only one possible solution.

To get started, scan the puzzle for each digit, starting with 1, to see if there are enough of them that you can fill in the rest. Then look for the rows, columns, or cages that have five or more numbers filled in to see if you can deduce where the others can be placed—with no guessing! After you have explored these possibilities, once again scan the puzzle for each number. This will give you a good starting point to test out hypotheses on number placement to solve the rest of the puzzle.

SUDOKU 1

ANSWER ON PAGE 125

							5	2
	4			3	7			9
		9	4			1	7	
			1	9			4	
		7				2		
	2			7	6			
	9	8			1	5		
4			9	2			8	
7	5							

GETTING STARTED WITH LOGIC PUZZLES

Brain Health Benefits

Logic puzzles can improve deductive reasoning, focus, and working memory. A logic puzzle requires you to use the facts presented in the clues to determine how people or items in various categories are related to each other. The first step is carefully reading the clues, trying not to miss important details. It can be quite challenging to remember details as you examine possible outcomes. And keep in mind the need to follow threads carefully: Even in a simple logic puzzle with four people, four makes of car, and four car colors, there are 64 possible combinations and in some of the tougher puzzles toward the end of this book there are 625 possible combinations to deal with. It's time for steely focus.

How to Solve

The key to solving logic puzzles is to eliminate possible outcomes until there is only one possible result left in each category. So read each clue to determine which possibilities can be eliminated (e.g., "John doesn't have the blue car"). There may also be positive statements, such as "Jessica likes her BMW."

Use of the logic grid is critical to solving the puzzle because it allows you to keep a visual tally of your deductions. You use it to check off invalid possibilities by filling the box with an X. Using the example above, you would write an X in the box that connects "John" and "blue car." In the other example, you could write an O in the box that connects "Jessica" and "BMW" and an X in each box that connects other names with Jessica's car.

 **PUZZLE ON NEXT PAGE**

FUN WITH PUZZLES

Four siblings share a love of puzzles, but each one likes a different sort of puzzle, and they prefer working on puzzles in different fashions. Let's review their puzzle-solving activities and see if you can sort out who solves which puzzles and when or where.

1. Adam, the eldest, doesn't enjoy crosswords or working on his puzzles while traveling or on weekends.

2. Denise, the youngest, really loves crosswords but, like Adam, doesn't work on them on weekends.

3. Neither of the two middle siblings, Bob and Carla, likes logic puzzles, and Carla digs into puzzles only when she is traveling.

4. The sibling who likes word searches enjoys doing them on weekends, and the logic puzzle fan won't think about them at all while at work.

ANSWER ON PAGE 125

	Crosswords	Sudoku	Logic puzzles	Word search	On work breaks	Evenings at home	Weekends	On travel
Adam								
Bob								
Carla								
Denise								
On work breaks								
Evenings at home								
Weekends								
On travel								

2

EASY PUZZLES

OPPOSITES ATTRACT

1	2	3	4	5	6		7	8	9	10		11	12	13
14							15					16		
17					18							19		
20				21					22	23				
		24					25	26						
27	28	29				30	31					32	33	
34				35		36				37				
38			39		40				41		42			
43		44		45				46		47				
48			49				50		51					
	52						53	54						
55	56				57					58	59	60		
61			62	63	64				65					
66			67				68							
69			70				71							

TRY THIS!
Write a list of words, do a puzzle, and without looking, try to recall the words. Do this sequence again with a longer list.

Across

1. Park structure with open sides
7. Uncouth sort
11. Heat measure: Init.
14. Newspaper biggie
15. In addition
16. ___ Angeles, CA
17. Cole Porter classic
19. Suffix with Canaan or Israel
20. Junior naval officer: Abbr.
21. Supporting rope
22. Confessed, with "up"
24. Large jug
25. Chose, with "for"
27. Iraqi port
30. Move around freely, be transitory
34. Daughter of Zeus and goddess of wisdom
36. Protestant denomination: Abbr.
37. Perfumed powder
38. Confucian path
39. Word opposite in meaning to another, of which we have some examples in each of 17, 30, 48, and 62 Across
42. Body art, for short
43. Gator's kin
45. Intense anger
46. Nero's tutor, or Iroquois tribe
48. Haphazard, disorganized
51. Beat (out) by a narrow margin
52. Inexpensive
53. Vier und vier
55. Razor sharpener
57. Field
58. *60 Minutes* network: Init.
61. Oolong, for one
62. _____ case (legal dispute in which the outcome is not in doubt)
66. Canine cry
67. Medical advice, often
68. Mother _____ of Calcutta
69. Mammal has three, modem has two
70. Cassette contents
71. Sounds of derision

Down

1. Heredity unit
2. Score after deuce, in tennis
3. Turns sharply
4. Biblical verb ending
5. Landlocked country in southern Africa
6. Declaim
7. ____ *and the Tramp* (2019 Disney remake)
8. Antiquated
9. Can. neighbor: Init.
10. Prius or Supra
11. Occasions when one goes out with someone they've never met
12. Lug, schlep
13. Brought into play
18. DEA agent, slangily
23. Left
24. Bard's "before"
25. Arabian sultanate
26. English diarist Samuel _____
27. Quantity of cookies
28. Pong's maker
29. Roll the dice for money
31. Double-reed instruments
32. Candied, as cherries
33. Scientific name for a group of eight
35. Soul: Lat.
40. Word following road or ego
41. Type of herring made into fish meal
44. Small salmon
47. Excluding
49. Student's assignment
50. ____ Lee (baked goods brand)
54. "Red" coins
55. Eye affliction
56. Kind of spirit or effort
57. Feed the kitty
58. Music legend who started out with Sonny
59. Boom's opposite
60. Amtrak stops: Abbr.
63. Potpie morsel
64. Clairvoyant's gift: Init.
65. Full house sign: Init.

ANSWER ON PAGE 125

THE FAB FIVE

DID YOU KNOW?

Physical exercise can boost brain health in many ways. It can make a person's heart beat faster, increase blood flow, and send oxygen to the brain. More oxygen is like a breath of fresh air! The brain likes it and can think more clearly.

Across

1. "C'___ la vie!"
4. Don Draper, and others
9. Owl sounds
14. Hide-hair connector
15. Establish as true
16. Relating to the forearm bone
17. It's between Miss. and Ga. on the map: Abbr.
18. Hindu queen
19. Mathematical comparison
20. *Famous Chicago avenue
22. Civil rights activist ___ Parks
23. In base 8
24. Varnish ingredient
26. Fink
29. Rampage, tumult
30. Atlantic food fish
31. Fries or baked beans, say
32. Good way to warm up
34. Ridicule, mock
36. Pro
37. Derisive shout
38. Difficult and tiring
42. Like cornrows
46. Christmas carol
47. No. Amer. flycatcher
49. Misplace
50. ___ Jam Recordings (rap label)
51. Make dim
52. Gossip, busybody: in Yiddish
53. *New York's ____ Canal
55. *Higher in quality
57. Talk a blue streak
59. See 64 Across
60. Charlotte-to-Raleigh direction: Init.
61. Moisten while cooking
62. Overweight
63. Bro's sib
64. With 59 Across, what the answers to the starred (*) clues are, when they are given a different meaning
65. Leans over, as a boat
66. Body art, for short

Down

1. Captivates
2. Make a pitch to get
3. Farmer's field vehicle
4. Fourth in the year
5. Party pooper
6. Crowned head of state
7. Carpenter's plane, e.g.
8. Maiden name preceder
9. *Tribe also known as Wyandot
10. Waves, in Oaxaca
11. *Ottawa's province
12. Mai ___ (rum cocktail)
13. "No seats left" initials
21. Really horrid, as a person
22. (Of a horse) easy to be a jockey on
25. Fa follower
27. Big fuss
28. Half a score
30. Moral doubt (usually used in the plural)
31. _____ alert ("Don't listen if you haven't seen the movie yet!")
33. As well
35. Extinct flightless bird
38. "What's more..."
39. Fish eggs
40. Part of DoD
41. Bishop's jurisdiction
42. Wigs worn in the 18th century
43. Most upscale
44. Baltic country
45. Honey, sweetie pie
48. Japanese horseradish
51. Stanford-_____ IQ test
52. Affirmatives
54. Duty roster (from the Latin)
56. Annoyance
57. She's said to be "notorious": Init.
58. Former Mideast org.: Init.
59. Texter's guffaw

ANSWER ON PAGE 125

PUNZAPALOOZA

1	2	3	4		5	6	7	8		9	10	11	12	13
14					15					16				
17				18						19				
20						21		22		23				
	24				25				26					
27	28			29	30			31						
32			33		34		35		36			37	38	39
40					41		42			43				
44				45			46			47				
		48			49		50		51		52			
53	54	55				56			57	58				
59					60			61				62	63	
64			65		66	67								
68					69					70				
71					72					73				

TRIVIA CHALLENGE
Which planet was named after the Roman goddess of love and beauty? Which was named after the Roman god of war?

ANSWER ON PAGE 124

Across

1. Illegal block, in football
5. Russian legislature
9. Ann ____, MI
14. First-rate: Hyphen.
15. JFK postings: Init.
16. Capital of Western Australia
17. To write with a broken pencil is _____
19. Athenian philosopher who taught Aristotle
20. Call for, involve
21. Prefix for shell or shore
23. Odd's opposite
24. ___-advised (unwise)
25. This girl said she recognized me from the Vegetarians Club, but I swear I've never met _____
27. Tax preparer, for short: Init.
29. Environmental prefix
31. *Gone with the Wind* plantation
32. 50%
34. Bullring cheer
36. A Beatle
40. Wrinkly citrus fruit that grows in the Caribbean
41. Back in?
43. Kind of phone or tower
44. Yellowstone's Old Faithful, e.g.
46. Pro's opposite
47. Decorative pitcher
48. Anagram for HULA
50. ___ *Misérables*
52. Cry audibly
53. England has no kidney bank, but it does have a _____.
57. Listening device or kind of dance
59. Febreze target
60. Chinese "way"
61. Ventilate
64. 1965 march site
66. Haunted French pancakes give me _____
68. Really bother
69. München mister
70. Semimonthly tide
71. What Pisa's tower does
72. ____ out (barely beat)
73. Major employer?

Down

1. What Count Dracula might wear on a chilly night
2. Aquatic bird
3. At first
4. Prison-related
5. Computer company headquartered in Round Rock, TX
6. Colorado Indian
7. En ____ (as a group)
8. Declare with confidence
9. Uber has one, so does Amazon
10. Pertinence or materiality
11. *Real Housewives* network
12. Aquatic mammal
13. Fr. river that flows into the Mediterranean
18. Type of roof
22. Mother-of-pearl source
25. Place for an ace
26. Anger
27. Muffled engine sound of a slow-moving boat
28. ____-turner (exciting book)
30. On the take
33. Angler
35. And so on: Abbr.
37. The *Times* or *Sun-Times*
38. Butter alternative
39. Fed. agency that enforces labor laws: Init.
42. Restaurant freebie
45. Corn unit
49. Detest
51. Suffix with gang or mob
53. Mislays
54. Best possible
55. He invented the electric battery
56. ____ and aahed
58. Madison Square Garden, e.g.
61. *God's Little* ___
62. ___ player (person who works well in a group)
63. Catch a glimpse of
65. Lawyer: Abbr.
67. Unit of work

ANSWER ON PAGE 125

HE PLAYS A ROLE

DID YOU KNOW?

Plenty of restful sleep is helpful throughout our lives, and especially helpful as we age.
While the brain isn't technically a muscle, it still needs "exercise," and then needs ample rest.
Get a decent night's sleep for many reasons, including an improved memory.

Across

1. Epiphany figures
5. Target and Wal-Mart competitor
10. 18th-century headgear
14. Clickable image
15. When Hamlet says, "The play's the thing..."
16. Flat and smooth
17. He gets top billing . . . or a hint to the starts of 26, 52, and 60 Across
19. U2 vocalist
20. "I had no ___!"
21. Funds held by a third party
23. Monks who can be found in 26 Across
26. Asian mountain range
29. Not "fer"
30. "___ Karenina," by Tolstoy
31. 911 responder: Init.
32. Forgo
34. Got bigger
36. Scull
39. Bro or sis
40. Conceal
42. Tiny, to a Scot
43. Okla. City–to–Tulsa direction: Init.
44. Diva's delivery
45. Venomous snakes
47. Whole ___ (holding nothing back)
49. Isn't wrong?
51. Habeas corpus, e.g.
52. Person called "duenna" in Spain
55. Diamond corners
56. Alter, correct
57. Plaintiff
59. Hip bones
60. Renovates and updates, as an old neighborhood
66. Opening for coins
67. Mayflower Compact signer
68. Barely beat (with "out")
69. Go (over) very closely
70. Fills, as a truck
71. Former Venetian official

Down

1. "Cool" amount
2. Duffer's dream
3. Former Portuguese colony on the Arabian Sea
4. Residents of 3 Down
5. *Citizen* ____ (classic Welles movie)
6. Trump's WH Counsel until Oct. 2018
7. 20's dispenser: Init.
8. Narrow inlet
9. Technical term for a certain skin problem
10. Skype tool
11. Places where people happily are cut off from the practicalities of life
12. Birthplace of Columbus
13. Precipitates the white stuff
18. Driver's license and others: Init.
22. Slid wildly, as a car on ice
23. Run out, as a subscription
24. From the top
25. Bad conduct
27. Firmly fix (an attitude) in a person (mostly used in the past tense)
28. Foal's mother
30. Mimic
33. Language conventions
35. Coup d'____
37. Eagle's nest
38. Gets some shut-eye
41. "Later"
46. Made (another) appear small in comparison
48. Narcotic
50. Fit one within another
52. Like fresh potato chips
53. Nametag word
54. Kingly
55. At, in Aachen
58. Big coffee dispensers
61. "Evil Woman" band, for short
62. Confidentiality contract: Init.
63. Bachelor's last words
64. Lay an ___ (bomb)
65. Discern, perceive

ANSWER ON PAGE 126

STRING QUARTET

Across

1. Banquet, lavish dinner
6. Away from port
10. "Quiet down!"
14. The _____ Incident (1943 classic Western starring Henry Fonda)
15. ["That was close!"]
16. Not fooled by
17. What some transparent wrappers are made of
19. Do in, as a dragon
20. Aloof
21. Get-out-of-jail money
22. Play for time
23. Expression meaning nonsense or utter foolishness made famous by Scarlett in GWTW
26. Mariner's maps
29. Hello, ____! (hit musical in the 1960s)
30. Well ventilated
31. Deli item
33. Chop (off)
36. Confederate soldier, for short
37. Wobbles
39. It might be added to impress
40. Last Greek consonant
41. Dog's tag datum
42. Slant, misrepresent
43. Pulled with a truck
45. Many ride Harleys
47. Town at the confluence of the Potomac and Shenandoah rivers
51. It sometimes is spam
52. Run ___ (go wild)
53. Pub quaff
56. Meter maid of song
57. Actor in Legally Blonde and Old School
60. Highlander
61. Consumer
62. Really bad, as weather
63. In this place
64. Indiana town close to Chicago
65. Must, slangily

Down

1. Central points (from the Latin)
2. The E in CEO: Abbr.
3. With competence
4. Fa follower
5. Small-time
6. Garden pest
7. "I ___ return"
8. Hallow ending
9. Amaze
10. Cheap lodging for traveling students
11. Not appropriate, as behavior, for a well-brought-up girl
12. No longer fresh
13. "According to _____" (orthodox, correct)
18. Hipster's word for residences
22. Hawks, markets
23. Word following stir or deep
24. Landscaper's tool
25. Person of action
26. Bellyache, complain
27. Goes quickly: Arch.
28. Person appointed to adjudicate a dispute
31. Curves, as in a road
32. Devoured
34. Partner of "done with"
35. Seats with kneelers
37. Spa handout
38. Decorative pitcher
42. Shade of blue
44. Narcotic
45. Facial feature
46. Getting under one's skin
47. Pulitzer-winning journalist Seymour _____
48. Liturgical vestment
49. Charlatan
50. Manicurist's _____ board
53. Helper: Abbr.
54. 1990's Senate majority leader
55. Irish singer
57. Haul, schlep
58. No. Amer. country: Init.
59. Neighbor of a Vietnamese

ANSWER ON PAGE 126

"I'M IMPRESSED"

TRIVIA CHALLENGE
Who was the first African American to play in
Major League Baseball?

ANSWER ON PAGE 124

Across

1. Get on, as a train
6. Work gang, ship's complement
10. Transport
14. Layabout
15. Zeus' wife
16. Shrek, for one
17. _____ National Preserve (scenic wetlands adjacent to the Everglades)
19. Badgers
20. Hilo feast
21. Elevator, to the Brits
22. Brimless cap
23. Surfaces
25. Articulate, utter
26. _____ National Park (Kentucky site that is a delight for spelunkers)
32. Coffee break snack
36. Large-scale musical work, like Handel's *Messiah*
37. Score after deuce, in tennis
38. _____ Banks (NC seaside area)
40. *Death in Venice* author
41. Twaddle, poppycock
43. French clerics
44. Spectacular Wyoming mountains near Jackson Hole
47. Commotion
48. Assert again
53. Irate
56. Grant and Lee, for two: Abbr.
58. Hip bones
59. Mined fuel
60. Eye-catching river site in Montana . . . or just north of Washington, D.C.
62. Wight or Man, e.g.
63. River deposit
64. Eat away
65. Colorized, as Easter eggs
66. Anagram for PEAS
67. Twisted about the vertical axis, as an airplane

ANSWER ON PAGE 126

Down

1. Book to swear on
2. Repugnance
3. Swimming pool problem
4. Happen again
5. Like some humor or martinis
6. Sacramental oil
7. Coral formation
8. While lead-in
9. Is in the past?
10. Beehive structure
11. Food thickener
12. Strongly encourage
13. "___ we forget . . ."
18. Nolo contendere, e.g.
22. Thai currency
24. Clock standard: Init.
25. *A ____ Is Born*
27. Short piece of sacred choral music
28. Bauxite, e.g.
29. Riyadh resident
30. Kudzu, for one
31. Ages and ages
32. "____ Me" (Roger Miller song)
33. Skunk's defense
34. Songstress ____ Simone
35. Disentangled
38. Able to see right through
39. Finish, with "up"
42. Mini whirlpool
43. Beast of burden
45. Elaborately decorated
46. Tree house?
49. Coronet
50. Permit
51. Squiggly accent mark
52. Lightened (up)
53. Battery fluid
54. Overly inquisitive
55. Battering wind
56. Grasp
57. Congers
60. Fed. property overseer: Init.
61. Tina ___ of *30 Rock* fame

ACTION NEEDED

IFZGKMU FZ ZFDXVU P XFQRQ KB XPXQM RKSQMQE

CFGI XMFOG; GIQ DPFO GIFON FZ ZGFVV GK DPTQ

IFZGKMU, OKG GK CMFGQ FG.

—XMFORQ KGGK SKO WFZDPMRT

HINTS (PAGE 124): 14, 1, 20
ANSWER ON PAGE 126

USING ONE'S NOODLE

TKZ UKNUAK DXVHL SNGK DXWH DZN NG DXGKK

DVSKF W CKWG. V XWBK SWJK WH VHDKGHWDVNHWA

GKUODWDVNH TNG SCFKAT RC DXVHLVHM NHQK NG

DZVQK W ZKKL.

—MKNGMK RKGHWGJ FXWZ

HINTS (PAGE 124): 6, 3, 16
ANSWER ON PAGE 126

IT DOESN'T TAKE AN ARMY

KPGPC EFLIU UJDU D HBDRR OCFLS FQ UJFLOJUQLR,

MFBBXUUPE MXUXNPKH MDK MJDKOP UJP TFCRE.

XKEPPE, XU XH UJP FKRA UJXKO UJDU PGPC JDH.

—BDCODCPU BPDE

HINTS (PAGE 124): 8, 9, 25
ANSWER ON PAGE 126

TRIPLE PLAY

P DKKI FGPI PVI DKKI FGPWM PWG PUJPNA P

SKWRXIPZUG HKRZXVPMXKV. ZQM JFGV NKQ PII MK

MFPM P UXMGWPMG MKVDQG KW EGV, MFGV NKQ

FPCG AKRGMFXVD CGWN AEGHXPU.

—VGUAKV RPVIGUP

HINTS (SEE PAGE 124): 4, 22, 31
ANSWER ON PAGE 126

WOMEN OF COUNTRY MUSIC

```
T V I H J L X N E N N A S O R
N A R R E K L J N M S P M K M
F T M E R P W L O A M R A K A
A S A M A E Y Y L D E Z N M R
Y N H T Y R T Q N T E L O U T
N Y S K E E T E R O C E S U I
A Y F H I T T A C A N A I O N
T P S N A E C S R G E N L L A
S W N Y I E H R Y A A A A Y A
Y O L T N A I K S H B J Q M D
B O T U N E I O T S E R F M N
R O J I Q T M M A I R E A E A
D S A T T E R O L R C F I B R
M Z Q Y L L O D F T Q K T N I
C U E I B B O B L Y N N H N M
```

ALISON Kraus

BARBARA mandrell

BOBBIE gentry

BONNIE raitt

CARRIE underwood

CRYSTAL gayle

DOLLY parton

DOTTIE west

EMMYLOU harris

FAITH hill

JANA kramer

JO DEE messina

JUNE CARTER cash

KITTY wells

LEANN rimes

LEE ANN womack

LORETTA lynn

LYNN anderson

MARTINA mcbride

MIRANDA lambert

PAM tillis

PATSY cline

REBA mcentire

ROSANNE cash

SHANIA twain

SHERYL crow

SKEETER davis

TAMMY wynette

TANYA tucker

TAYLOR swift

TERRI clark

TRISHA yearwood

WYNONNA judd

ANSWER ON PAGE 126

CAREGIVER QUALITIES

```
T E C N P D E T O V E D P I V
N H S D W R T G G F S A T H T
G A O I E P A N N U T L G O S
N U I U W P I Y O I G R E P R
I V N R G R E R E N V F N E Z
D L J S A H E N I R S O T F E
N T U C E N T V D M F R L U V
A U X F E L I F I A O U E L I
T T R G P G F L U B N L Z T
S O Z S R L I I P L F L D T C
R R J O E N E U S I B O E E E
E L F E G W S H G H C L D E T
D E T R A E H T F O S S N W O
N K O O C D O O G V E Z I S R
U V R O L E S N U O C I K D P
```

CARING	GENTLE	PATIENT	THOUGHTFUL
COUNSELOR	GOOD COOK	PRAYERFUL	TUTOR
DEPENDABLE	HELPFUL	PROTECTIVE	UNDERSTANDING
DEVOTED	HOPEFUL	SMILING	UNSELFISH
DISCIPLINARIAN	KIND	SOFTHEARTED	WISE
FORGIVING	LOVING	SUPPORTER	
GENEROUS	NURSE	SWEET	ANSWER ON PAGE 126

VALENTINE'S DAY

```
B I W T F O S M E O P S V U R
S E M C X A F E H L T O H M E
E D M Y Y L S Q C N D C J U N
M R P Y O S X E E N O D L S N
Y K E W V U W M S O A H U I I
H S E N L A R E M O K M U C D
R R J O G A L S E I R E O I T
S C V D E A R E S T V D S R I
T E H D A C P S N O I B E O L
R E N E J R E M L T U E Y R E
A E A Q R S L E A R I D U C L
E R O M A I U I E H N N A U D
H U G S O R S H N A C A E P N
T F I G T V C H C G R E B I A
D R A C G N I T E E R G Q D C
```

AMORE	CUPID	"I'M YOURS"	SMOOCH
"BE MY VALENTINE"	DARLING	KISSES	SWEETIE
BEAU	DEAREST	LOVE	"TE AMO"
CANDLELIT DINNER	ENDEARMENTS	MUSIC	TRUE LOVE
CANDY	FLOWERS	POEM	
CHAMPAGNE	GIFT	RED ROSES	ANSWER ON PAGE 126
CHERISH	GREETING CARD	RHYMES	
CHERUBS	HEARTS	ROMANCE	
CUDDLE	HUGS	"SAY YES"	

PLACES TO GO SKIING

```
M R F N O T G N I L L I K R S
U O N G S N O W B I R D B K S
S A N Q M K P S I W W J I E A
B T U T E Z R B V H A P G Y P
S L R M T T A D I A K D S S E
S A O A A R S T U G I R K T I
A V D O T T E S S R R L Y O M
P W X N O T N M N A A O H N L
N H H W A O O I B L H N C E A
O O E I W L K N A L A S G K U
T O L S S C E E W R A E T O Q
E D H Y E T R V O H C N H M O
T O A R X O L D O Y F Z T N N
E O B F B D L E R L T A O S S
N E P S A E Y B R O M L E Y A
```

ALTA
ASPEN
BIG ROCK
BIG SKY
BOREAL
BRECKINRIDGE
BROMLEY
BRYCE

DURANGO
ELDORA
HOODOO
KEYSTONE
KILLINGTON
LOVELAND
MONT TREMBLANT
MT SHASTA

OKEMO
SNOQUALMIE PASS
SNOWBIRD
SNOWSHOE
STOWE
STRATTON
TAOS
TETON PASS

VAIL
WHISTLER
WHITETAIL
WISP

ANSWER ON PAGE 126

POPCORN

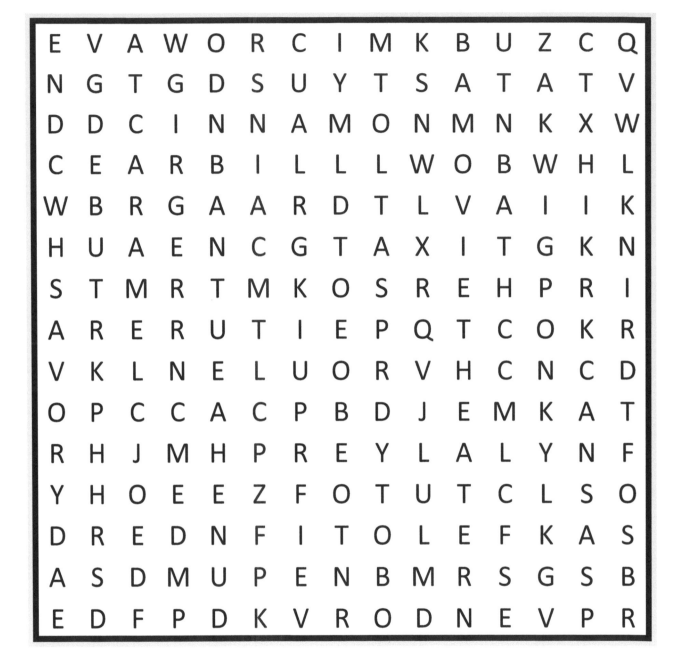

E	V	A	W	O	R	C	I	M	K	B	U	Z	C	Q
N	G	T	G	D	S	U	Y	T	S	A	T	A	T	V
D	D	C	I	N	N	A	M	O	N	M	N	K	X	W
C	E	A	R	B	I	L	L	W	O	B	W	H	L
W	B	R	G	A	A	R	D	T	L	V	A	I	I	K
H	U	A	E	N	C	G	T	A	X	I	T	G	K	N
S	T	M	R	T	M	K	O	S	R	E	H	P	R	I
A	R	E	R	U	T	I	E	P	Q	T	C	O	K	R
V	K	L	N	E	L	U	O	R	V	H	C	N	C	D
O	P	C	C	A	C	P	B	D	J	E	M	K	A	T
R	H	J	M	H	P	R	E	Y	L	A	L	Y	N	F
Y	H	O	E	E	Z	F	O	T	U	T	C	L	S	O
D	R	E	D	N	F	I	T	O	L	E	F	K	A	S
A	S	D	M	U	P	E	N	B	M	R	S	G	S	B
E	D	F	P	D	K	V	R	O	D	N	E	V	P	R

AIR-POPPED	CHEESE	MUNCHY	TASTY
AROMA	CINNAMON	PUFFED	TUB
BAG	CRACKERJACKS	REC ROOM	VENDOR
BALL	KERNAL	SALT	WHITE
BOWL	KETTLE CORN	SAVORY	
BUTTERED	LIGHT	SNACK	ANSWER ON PAGE 127
CANOLA OIL	MICROWAVE	SOFT DRINK	
CARAMEL	MOVIE THEATER	STRING	

PORTMANTEAU WORDS

```
T  I  X  E  R  B  O  M  N  T  K  R  A  N  S
R  E  B  Z  R  T  B  Z  A  B  S  E  I  C  N
O  M  M  Q  M  I  G  R  W  P  A  G  T  R  M
K  O  O  O  O  E  C  O  O  M  S  I  X  O  O
S  J  S  P  T  O  D  R  X  M  B  L  T  N  Y
C  I  I  N  I  K  I  S  U  A  E  S  U  W
H  C  T  H  G  S  C  P  C  Z  L  N  V  T  G
O  V  C  I  X  O  A  O  A  A  Z  A  C  F  I
R  E  O  W  S  N  M  M  N  R  R  V  Z  E  N
T  B  M  P  G  E  C  S  K  L  J  E  C  D  O
L  L  L  L  J  D  O  O  W  Y  L  L  O  B  R
E  A  I  O  D  H  I  R  E  N  E  E  W  T  M
Y  S  X  A  L  L  I  H  C  Q  U  B  I  T  O
H  E  T  T  E  U  Q  I  T  E  N  E  A  S  U
E  R  A  C  A  M  A  B  O  M  E  D  O  M  S
```

BIOPIC	CRONUT	MOTEL	SPAM
BOLLYWOOD	EMOJI	NETIQUETTE	SPANGLISH
BREXIT	EMOTICON	OBAMACARE	SPORK
BROMANCE	GINORMOUS	QUBIT	TECHNOCRAT
CHILLAX	LIGER	SKORT	TWEENER
CHORTLE	MEDICARE	SMOG	
COSPLAY	MODEM	SNARK	ANSWER ON PAGE 127

ROCK AND ROLL HALL OF FAME

```
G M E X P T Q G N I K B B C A
W A E J E C E C N I R P O B F
H I V T R R W K H S I P B B S S
S V L E A O T I E E M A D A N
U U A S Q L D S A L U E Y M E
R M D P O C L S R G D D L C L
T D T R S N A I T A D A A O A
S O W I J N P S C E Y W N O V
K N Z Z T O P I E A W N Z K E
N O R A B O H N C O A A X E I
I V N U H K A N N K T R R R H
K A D W Q U E E N I E B X T C
E N E I D R T U V M R T O Q T
H H J F O U R T O P S L T O I
T M A D O N N A N A V R I N R
```

ABBA	**FOUR TOPS**	**PRINCE**	**T. REX**
B.B. KING	**HEART**	**QUEEN**	**THE KINKS**
BOB DYLAN	**KISS**	**R.E.M.**	**THE WHO**
CREAM	**MADONNA**	**RITCHIE VALENS**	**WILSON PICKETT**
DONOVAN	**METALLICA**	**ROD STEWART**	**ZZ TOP**
DR. JOHN	**MUDDY WATERS**	**RUSH**	
DUANE EDDY	**N.W.A.**	**SAM COOKE**	**ANSWER ON PAGE 127**
EAGLES	**NIRVANA**	**SANTANA**	

CALCUDOKU 2

ANSWER ON PAGE 127

1	12×	6×	
12×		5+	1-
	2:		
2		1-	

CALCUDOKU 3

ANSWER ON PAGE 127

3	4×		3+
2	5+	1-	
4×			1-
	1-		

CALCUDOKU 4

ANSWER ON PAGE 127

1-		1	12+	
3+		4		6×
9+		3:		
4+	12+	2-		8+

CALCUDOKU 5

ANSWER ON PAGE 127

7+		9+		4:
	6+	2-	5+	
8+				5
		2-	8×	
20×				3

CALCUDOKU 6

ANSWER ON PAGE 127

8×	1-		5	3:
	4-		2:	
5:	10+			24×
		2:		
3			9+	

CALCUDOKU 7

ANSWER ON PAGE 127

8+		4	5:	2×
4	2-	1-		
5+			6×	9+
		11+		
2			7+	

SUDOKU 2

ANSWER ON PAGE 128

3		5				2		
		9	2			1	7	
2					9		8	3
			4	7		3		
	1						5	
		2		5	1			
5	2		1					8
	9	4			8	7		
		7				4		5

SUDOKU 3

ANSWER ON PAGE 128

	6	8			7		9	
						5		6
		4	8		5			
					8			
7		9				2		3
			5					
			1		9	4		
4		7						
	1		2			3	7	

SUDOKU 4

ANSWER ON PAGE 128

	1			4	2	6		
		2			3		1	
		7	6					4
		8		6				
6			3		4			8
				7		5		
8					5	3		
	3		1			2		
		6	9	3			8	

SUDOKU 5

ANSWER ON PAGE 128

4						7	2	
	8		6	7			3	
			5		1			8
		3		5			6	
	5			4		8		
6			3		7			
	3			1	8		4	
	7	1						3

SUDOKU 6

ANSWER ON PAGE 128

			6		2			
2	3	5						
		4	3	5		2		
		3		9			7	
	7		2		6		9	
	9			1		5		
		9		6	5	8		
						9	3	4
			9		7			

SUDOKU 7

ANSWER ON PAGE 128

			7					9
					8	3	5	
3	4	8	6					7
					6			5
9	6						2	3
5			2					
2					5	6	3	8
	3	5	9					
8				4				

VACATION PLANS

With summer approaching, four coworkers are discussing their plans for annual vacations. They all have great plans, but they couldn't be more different. From the clues given, see if you can figure out who is going where and doing what.

1. Jim is not going to Southeast Asia and won't be backpacking or visiting friends.

2. The person planning to backpack, who isn't Jackie, will be somewhere else besides Europe.

3. Jane plans to spend all of her vacation time in South America but not backpacking or visiting friends; Joe will skip New England.

4. The European sojourner won't be visiting friends or staying at a resort.

ANSWER ON PAGE 128

	Southeast Asia	Europe	New England	South America	At a resort	Guided tour	Backpacking	Visiting friends
Jackie								
Jane								
Jim								
Joe								
At a resort				
Guided tour				
Backpacking				
Visiting friends				

SANDWICH PLATTERS

Joe's Diner is known for the wide variety of delicious sandwich platters it offers at lunchtime. In fact, there are four platters sitting on the counter right now, waiting to be served to hungry customers. From the clues given, see if you can figure out, without being there, what has gone into each platter—meat, bread, and side. One of them might whet your appetite enough to send you to the kitchen to make up your own platter.

1. The ham was served either on the whole wheat or ciabatta bread but not with coleslaw.

2. The roast beef came with French fries but wasn't served on whole wheat.

3. Joe doesn't think potato salad or pastrami mix well with pita bread, so neither of those combos are on the menu, but the pastrami wasn't served on sourdough bread, either.

4. The turkey sandwich, which was not on sourdough bread, came with chips.

5. Ciabatta bread was not used to make the pastrami sandwich.

ANSWER ON PAGE 128

	Sourdough	Whole wheat	Pita bread	Ciabatta	Coleslaw	Corn chips	French fries	Potato salad
Ham								
Roast beef								
Pastrami								
Turkey								
Coleslaw								
Corn chips								
French fries								
Potato salad								

MEETING SCHEDULE

It looks like Linda Lawyer is going to have a busy afternoon, as she has agreed to four meetings with clients on four different topics. With the clues provided about these appointments as she described them to her assistant, maybe we can help the assistant set up the meeting schedule and prepare the documents needed for the meetings.

1. Claude called and got scheduled immediately following the meeting for his wife, Cloris, who wants her will revised, and can't meet after 2:30.

2. Neither Claude nor Cletus has a traffic ticket problem to be dealt with.

3. Clara said she can't meet after 4:00, as did the client who wants a small business incorporated.

4. The client with the traffic ticket issue has a conflict and can't be scheduled for 3:00.

ANSWER ON PAGE 128

	Contract	Incorporation	Traffic Ticket	Will	2:00	2:30	3:00	4:15
Clara								
Claude								
Cletus								
Cloris								
2:00								
2:30								
3:00								
4:15								

BARBECUE COOK-OFF

The final competition of the national barbecue cook-off has four contestants, each from a well-known center of barbecue cooking—Texas, Kansas City, Memphis, and North Carolina. With the help of the clues, see if you can sort out which contestant is from which part of the country, and which specialty they are going to whip up for the judges. Yum yum!

1. The barbecue cook preparing pulled pork, oddly enough, is not from North Carolina, nor is Bryant, who decided against cooking up baby back ribs.

2. The chef who is a woman grew up in Texas but moved away as a child. She is not a fan of baby back ribs.

3. Buck, who does not hail from Kansas City or Memphis, is doing barbecued beef ribs.

4. Neither Billy Bob nor Bryant are Memphis cooks, and the North Carolinian is not barbecuing baby back ribs.

5. The Texas cook is not smoking beef brisket or baby back ribs.

ANSWER ON PAGE 128

	Kansas City	Memphis	North Carolina	Texas	Baby back ribs	Beef brisket	Beef ribs	Pulled pork
Beulah								
Billy Bob								
Bryant								
Buck								
Baby back ribs								
Beef brisket								
Beef ribs								
Pulled pork								

HOUSE HUNTING

It is the start of the spring housing market, and Ron Realtor has been contacted by four potential buyers in the market for housing. They all differ in the key feature they are looking for in a house, and each wants a different financing arrangement. From the clues given, let's help Ron match everyone up with the house of their dreams.

1. Neither of Ron's clients who are couples are interested in the 5-year variable rate financing.

2. Ollie, who is not looking for a swimming pool or an extra bedroom, wants to finance for a shorter period than Marian, who wants a longer term loan than the client interested in a pool.

3. The prospective buyer who wants to lock in a 15-year fixed rate mortgage needs a place with an extra bedroom.

4. The potential buyer looking for a large backyard doesn't want a 1-year variable loan, and the prospect who wants to have a pool doesn't want to take on a 5-year variable rate loan.

5. Hal and Hallie, with two small kids, want a house close to schools.

ANSWER ON PAGE 128

	Near schools	Big backyard	Swimming pool	Extra bedroom	1-year variable	5-year variable	15-year fixed	30-year fixed
Hal and Hallie								
Ollie								
Marian								
Ed and Ellie								
1-year variable								
5-year variable								
15-year fixed								
30-year fixed								

MEDIUM PUZZLES

WE'VE GOT YOUR NUMBER

Across

1. Quarterback's primary go-to play
5. Man's name perhaps appropriate for someone in debt
9. Jordan's capital
14. Crowning point
15. Where the Vatican is
16. Jungle vine
17. Led the way, launched
19. Luxury make of car, slangily
20. Flap
21. Part in a play
22. "___ la la!"
23. Modern version of some pre-Christian religions
25. Beach sight, occasionally
30. Make a straight downhill run on skis (from the German)
32. Ump's call
33. Coffee server
34. Did a tape chore
37. On the briny
38. 2016 movie about some underappreciated NASA math whizzes, or a hint as to what is in the circled squares
41. Mother Teresa, and others
42. Bishopric
43. Word before Faithful or Glory
44. "Wait a ___!"
45. Beach footwear
49. What is experienced in Portland a lot
53. Speedometer or tachometer, e.g.
54. Doublemint, e.g.
55. Brown rival
57. Treat like a dog?
58. Pipsqueak
60. Adamant
62. Intuit
63. Got up
64. Commedia dell'___ (early form of theater originating in Italy)
65. O'Toole, Frampton, or Fonda
66. Breyer's rival
67. Cold War initials

Down

1. Melon-like tropical fruits
2. Like vinegar
3. Lock lips
4. Capitol Hill VIP: Abbr.
5. Creme-filled cookie
6. It precedes Series or Cup
7. Mideast VIP
8. ___ Beatty or Buntline
9. *Little Women* author Louisa May _____
10. Cat's cry
11. Scene of extreme confusion or uproar
12. Common conjunction
13. Aye's opposite
18. Expunged
24. Nursery rhyme food
26. Style of column in ancient Greece
27. ____ the truth (spins a bit of a yarn)
28. Bonanza finds
29. Genetic stuff: Init.
31. Its flag is a gold cross on a field of blue
35. In reserve
36. E.T.'s craft: Init.
37. Madison Square Garden, e.g.
38. Maui dance
39. Poor, needy
40. Language conventions
41. Common conjunction
44. Smile affectedly
46. Tricksters
47. Go-betweens
48. Missive
50. Surgeon's assistant
51. Church council
52. Impudent
56. Prevaricates
58. Cooking measure: Abbr.
59. Minuscule, to a Scot
60. Ill temper
61. It follows sigma

ANSWER ON PAGE 129

IN THE SWIM OF THINGS

1	2	3	4	5		6	7	8	9			10	11	12
13						14					15			
16				17						18				
19				20				21		22				
		23	24			25						26		
27	28				29	30				31	32			
33			34					35						
36						37					38	39	40	
		41				42								
43	44	45			46				47					
48			49	50			51	52						
53		54				55				56	57	58		
59				60	61			62						
63			64				65							
66			67				68							

DID YOU KNOW?

Keeping as healthy as possible is good for body and brain.
Medical conditions and medications can affect thinking and memory.
Talk to a healthcare provider if you notice changes.

Across

1. Crosswise, on a ship
6. _____ theft (computer crime)
10. Golfers' org.: Init.
13. Sheriff's group
14. Cracked open, as a door
15. Stylish
16. One of four swimming styles used in competitions
18. Saucy
19. Amtrak stop: Abbr.
20. "___ to worry"
21. Wraps around
23. Get ready for surgery
25. Pinocchio, at times
26. Arafat's org.: Init.
27. Type of collar or market
29. Norman port
31. *Barnaby Jones* star
33. At bottom
35. ___ Today
36. It's considered the fastest frontal swimming style
41. Fully anesthetized
42. Compels compliance, as with a law
43. Native New Zealander
46. Growl: Arch.
47. Like most cakes
48. Old common market inits.
49. "Phooey!"
51. Woodwind
53. Piece of bedroom furniture
55. High card
56. "Live Free or ___" (NH state motto)
59. _____ *Land* (2016 movie musical)
60. Type of swimming involving equipment
63. Harrow rival
64. It's six years for a senator
65. Sonata section
66. "Are we there ___?"
67. Legalese for postponement
68. Cheap 1980s auto imports

Down

1. Police dept. alerts, for short
2. Gravy ____ (piece of tableware)
3. Fugitives
4. Inquire
5. Old legal word for "middle"
6. Feathered missile
7. Garlic, in Granada
8. Give shelter to
9. *Gladiator* setting
10. Swimmer with 23 Olympic golds as of 2016
11. Undergarment that shapes the figure
12. Follows, as advice
15. Navy rank similar to Sgt.: Init.
17. Cold weather wear
22. *The Last Supper*, e.g.
24. Bird of prey, or member of the NBA's 2019 championship team
25. Merciful, as a judge
27. Food safety org.: Init.
28. Romanian money
30. Cobbler's tool
32. Hispanic district
34. Stonehenge worshippers
35. Remove from the priesthood
37. Santa ___, Calif.
38. Bowing (to)
39. Itsy-bitsy
40. Hallucinogenic init.
43. Competition that combines swimming styles
44. Make fizzy
45. Spotted wildcat
46. January's birthstone
50. Catches one's breath
52. Like many a frat party
54. Japanese honorific
55. Big football rival of Navy
57. Prefix with China
58. They can be inflated
61. Mouths, anatomically
62. ___ Reed or Rawls

ANSWER ON PAGE 129

DROP-DOWN MENU

TRY THIS!
Turn to a puzzle to take your mind off thoughts
that you find stressful.

Across

1. Western state: Abbr.
6. Juilliard degrees: Init.
10. Many miles away, poetically
14. Tiny organism
15. *Othello* villain
16. ____ down (reduce in size incrementally)
17. Deli staple
18. Secluded valley
19. "Not guilty," e.g.
20. Sandbars under the surface of the water
22. ____ through (skim, as a book)
24. Once around the track
25. Sal ____ (1950s movie star)
27. "Toodle-oo!"
29. American army that fought in WWI: Init.
32. Said twice, an Orkan greeting
33. Westernmost state
36. Record label until 2003: Init.
37. Courage and resolve
38. Doozies
39. Permitted
41. Doesn't use a trash can
43. Latin dance
44. Gambling game
45. Suffix with stamp or imp
46. They make you stand tall
48. Crowning
49. Dec. LA clock setting: Init.
50. ____ Coward (Eng. playwright)
51. Stalin's predecessor
53. Hair goo
55. Streamlet
57. Like most bread
61. Commotions
63. ____ through (skim, as a book)
65. Dried coconut meat
66. Not prerecorded
67. Burden
68. In-box item
69. Goulash
70. Votes in opposition
71. Scorch

Down

1. Taxis
2. Chinese nurse
3. Toy building block
4. Construction girder
5. Iconic Frank Lloyd Wright house
6. Russian fighter
7. Repercussions, or a platoon leader's order dismissing his or her troops
8. *A Death in the Family* writer
9. Beethoven's *Moonlight* ____
10. Snapchat or Instagram
11. Nod off
12. Length x width, for a rectangle
13. Harvest
21. Trap
23. "I _____" (Patsy Cline megahit)
26. Grain storage hub in Oklahoma
28. Not slack
29. Accumulate
30. Panache
31. Be smitten
34. Western Asia ethnic group
35. Valuable thing
40. Capital on a fjord
41. Overdue
42. O. Henry specialty
44. Patsy
47. Loafer or boat shoe, e.g.
52. Judd or Watts
53. Female hoedown participants
54. Polish for publication
56. ____ Turner (1940s and 1950s movie star)
58. Reach across
59. H.S. math class, for short
60. Ivy League school
62. Stitch up
64. Serpentine letter

ANSWER ON PAGE 129

TRIPLE PLAY

1	2	3	■	4	5	6	7	8	9	■	10	11	12	13
14				15						■	16			
17			18							■	19			
20					■	21			■	22				
■			23		24		■	25	26			27		
28	29	30		■	31		32	■	33		34			
35				36				■	37			■		
38				■	39		40	■	41		42	43	44	
■			45		46		■	47	48					
49	50	51				■	52			■	53			
54			■	55		56		57		58				
59			60		■	61	62		■	63		64	65	66
67				■	68			69						
70				■	71					■	72			
73				■	74					■	75			

DID YOU KNOW?

Changing your routine can be good for your brain. Try cooking new recipes.
Take a walk using a new route. Listen to music or an audiobook while you do your chores.
Doing routine tasks in new ways can strengthen the brain's ability to focus.

Across

1. Smartphone buy
4. _____ Street (where to find Big Bird)
10. Danny Ocean's wife, in the films
14. Fish eggs
15. Entrenched defensive position (from the So. Afr. Dutch)
16. Twain river rafter, familiarly
17. Also on the bill in an important role
19. Site of the Taj Mahal
20. (With 21 and 22 Across) brief and to the point
21. See 20 Across
22. See 20 Across
23. Brings into play
25. Be in session
27. Born, in Bordeaux
28. Arabian sultanate
31. Neither's partner
33. Baltimore footballers
35. Bacon, in Bologna
37. Genesis name
38. (With 39 and 41 Across) experimental process in which you try different approaches until hitting on the best
39. See 38 Across
41. See 38 Across
45. Beginning spot in golf
47. Large Australian city
49. Steal
52. Nay's opposite
53. Anagram for MITE
54. Drenched
55. 2003 Will Ferrell film
57. *M*A*S*H* actor
59. (With 61 and 63 Across) repeatedly
61. See 59 Across
63. See 59 Across
67. Guitarist Lofgren
68. More of a liking (for)
70. Forbidding or stern, as an expression
71. Make certain
72. Stranded motorist's need
73. Anatomical pouches
74. Certificates of ownership for cars
75. Connections, informally

Down

1. Circle parts
2. Winnie-the-____
3. Cancún coin
4. Blind parts
5. Corn unit
6. Florida home of the Ringling Museum of Art
7. Not "fer"
8. Heals
9. Work unit
10. Defrost
11. Home of the U. of Oregon
12. Type of door or pass
13. Glides on ice
18. Curtail, dock
22. _____ off (averts)
24. Tolkien creature
26. EU member: Abbr.
28. Pick, with "for"
29. Equinox month: Abbr.
30. *Wheel of Fortune* buy
32. Cleared or checked with
34. Excessive words
36. Number of players on a soccer team
40. Terrible
42. Fink
43. "We're number ___!"
44. Sleep acronym
46. Slithery swimmer
48. Suffix with mart or part
49. Banjo sounds
50. Exodus or migration (so named after Muhammad's flight from Mecca)
51. Slanted font
56. Persian language
58. Challenges
60. Doctrines
62. Cozy home
64. Prefix for freeze or septic
65. Clickable image
66. Part of CNN
68. Frisk, with "down"
69. "Able was I ___ . . ."

ANSWER ON PAGE 129

GET YOUR BEARINGS

1	2	3	4		5	6	7	8	9		10	11	12	13
14					15						16			
17				18							19			
20							21		22					
		23				24								
25	26	27				28			29			30	31	32
33				34				35		36				
37			38		39				40		41			
42				43		44				45		46		
47				48		49				50				
			51			52			53					
54	55	56					57				58	59	60
61					62	63							
64					65					66			
67					68					69			

TRIVIA CHALLENGE

Who gave a speech titled "Solitude of Self" to appeal for women's rights in 1892?

ANSWER ON PAGE 124

Across

1. Sudden fancy
5. That is, in Latin
10. Baby's first word, maybe
14. Top-of-the-line
15. Score-keeping position in duplicate bridge
16. "___ go bragh!"
17. Polo shirt, tennis shorts, running shoes, etc.
19. Escritoire
20. Antarctic bird
21. David's foe
23. Antiquity, once
24. Person who says, "Yeah, right"
25. Calif. city near the Mexican border
29. Got older
33. QB Manning
34. Ad for a TV show, for short
36. Place for NBA games
37. Adam ____ (1960s Batman portrayer)
39. They come after Augs.: Abbr.
41. ____ Carolina U., in Greenville
42. Fencing swords
44. Speaks, as the King James version would phrase it
46. Regret
47. Horned African beasts
49. Showed, as a movie
51. After-bath powders
53. Common conjunction
54. Tropical malady treated with quinine
57. Driver's or liquor _____
61. Sweeping tale
62. Betrothal
64. Fishing rod attachment
65. Anagram for SHOUT
66. Met solo
67. Marine eagle
68. Doctrinal principle
69. Absorbs, with "up"

Down

1. Bee's cousin
2. Rhode Island's motto
3. Get ___ the ground floor
4. Combined
5. Those with access to non-public information
6. Word following buckle or hunker
7. Before, to the poet
8. Excessively theatrical
9. Large crowd
10. Federal health program
11. Field
12. Atomizer output
13. Egyptian cross
18. Garden bulb
22. Turkish money
24. Directional device, the primary points of which can be found at appropriate spots in the grid
25. Underground drain
26. First Hebrew letter
27. Japanese American
28. "Here ____ nothing"
30. Long (for)
31. Follow
32. Old hat
35. Ear-related
38. Animal's long appendage
40. Opposite of crooked or winding
43. Fly high
45. Beginning of a conclusion
48. Most cunning
50. Swellings
52. Men's fragrance brand since 1936
54. Trifling
55. Mimic
56. Security for a debt
57. Overdue
58. Adopted son of Claudius
59. Barbershop sound
60. JFK postings: Init.
63. Rev, as an engine

ANSWER ON PAGE 129

GOOD LOCATIONS

TRY THIS!

Do you have a habit you're trying to break? Next time you have that urge, do a puzzle instead.

Across

1. Stringed instrument
5. Movie star _____ Berry
10. Charades, essentially
14. D-Day beach
15. Astrological ram
16. Organic compound
17. Situation that is very comfortable, colloquially
19. Play opener
20. Ballet wear
21. Philly team
23. Subatomic particle
26. Fictional Himalayan valley that is an earthly paradise
29. *Grand Theft* _____
30. Ship's bottom
31. Velvet finish?
32. Paper fastener
34. Word before flakes or chowder
36. Lawyers' group: Init.
39. .0000001 joule
40. As a substitute
42. Little 'un
43. Hawaiian floral necklace
44. Pepsi, e.g.
45. Swine-like animals
47. To the ___ degree (extremely)
49. Mars, to the Greeks
51. Excellent
52. State of complete happiness, colloquially
55. Sleep disorder
56. Not blown away by
57. Madcap
59. Turkish currency unit
60. State of financial comfort, colloquially
66. Taiwanese electronics giant
67. Decorative feather
68. Golden rule preposition
69. Airplane assignment
70. Fork prongs
71. Coal stratum

Down

1. Busy airport
2. Absorbed, as a cost
3. "Far out!"
4. Red carpet appearance, typically
5. Male deer
6. Stir up
7. Fleur-de-___
8. Confederate general
9. Krupp works city
10. Paltry, on Pall Mall
11. Tendency
12. Traveler's stop
13. Shortened form of the name of a certain reigning royal
18. Lighthearted pleasure
22. Meeting "to do" list
23. Swiss border city
24. Violating convention (from the French)
25. Assembly point
27. Metric land measure equal to 2.47 acres
28. Hand cream ingredient
30. Gambling game similar to lotto
33. Chinese fruit: Var.
35. "Darn!"
37. Carried
38. Befuddled
41. Czech or Serb, e.g.
46. Ancient form of paper
48. Stymie
50. Pepsin, e.g.
52. Hawaiian dances
53. In reserve
54. Skilled
55. Aardvark's morsel
58. Suffixes used in the names of some 50 Downs
61. *Aladdin* prince
62. Nearest star to Earth
63. Memphis-to-Nashville dir.: Init.
64. Greek *H*
65. Hanks or Cruise

ANSWER ON PAGE 129

LITERALLY SPEAKING

1	2	3	4		5	6	7	8		9	10	11	12	13
14					15					16				
17				18						19				
20							21	22						

DID YOU KNOW?

Challenging yourself to master a new skill can sharpen your brain and improve your memory.
Take up a new instrument, learn to knit or crochet, or do puzzle games.
Learning makes neural pathways stronger, and this is good.

Across

1. Indonesian island visited by many tourists
5. Not hearing
9. Poisonous shrub
14. Algerian port
15. Hindu princess
16. Being chilled, in anticipation of the party starting soon
17. Collection of wild animals
19. Runs in neutral
20. Someone or something you want to avoid, colloquially
21. Diatribes
23. German industrial city
24. Stadium section
25. Charitable flea-markety event
32. Small pieces used in the construction of a mosaic (with a Latinate ending)
36. Like some renewable energy
37. ___ *Brockovich*
38. Sprawls relaxedly
41. Cut of beef
42. Improvise
44. People who pay for a room and meals
46. Capable of being saved and fixed
49. *Idylls of the King* lady
50. Monikers
55. Ocean shipping route
58. Type of cable used with computers and TVs
60. Spice used in chili
61. When one is no longer a spring chicken but still not old . . . or what the answers to 17, 25, and 46 Across all have
63. Madison Square Garden, e.g.
64. "I cannot tell ___"
65. Handed-down history
66. Griller's utensil
67. Enjoys Vail or Aspen
68. Cooking fat

Down

1. Frozen dome-shaped dessert
2. Regions
3. Sets down, as a plane
4. Silly
5. Fictional young detective Nancy ____
6. Canal zones?
7. "Gimme ___!" (part of a U. of Miami cheer)
8. Celebratory get-together, in Guadalajara
9. Evening parties (from the French)
10. Beat the competitor's price
11. Eight furlongs
12. Got 100 on
13. Ex-, ac-, or re- finisher
18. Category, as of novels
22. A Marlboro or Kent, for short
26. WWW address: Init.
27. Cultural Revolution leader
28. Kind of toast
29. Balm ingredient
30. Animal's den or burrow
31. Coastal raptors
32. Afternoon socials
33. *Das Rheingold* goddess
34. Window ledge
35. In tears
39. Easy, high-arced throw
40. Actor Mineo
43. Easily peeled fruits
45. Kidney-related
47. Martini ingredient
48. Swellings
51. Skating jumps
52. Cat's cry
53. Tidal flood
54. Frozen rain
55. "Shoo!"
56. Continental coin
57. Augusta's ____ Corner
58. CCI x II
59. Keats creations
62. Kind, sort

ANSWER ON PAGE 129

OFF-SEASON BLUES

EPVEBP QNI TP RWQG M FV MK GWP RMKGPA RWPK

GWPAP'N KV OQNPOQBB. M'BB GPBB LVH RWQG

M FV. M NGQAP VHG GWP RMKFVR QKF RQMG

DVA NEAMKX.

—AVXPAN WVAKNOL

HINTS (SEE PAGE 124): 32, 5
ANSWER ON PAGE 129

WHAT COMES FIRST

OQNDXTM YG FVM WQGF YWAQDFXIF QL XKK FVM

ZYDFNMG JMOXNGM BYFVQNF OQNDXTM, PQN OXI'F

ADXOFYOM XIP QFVMD ZYDFNM OQIGYGFMIFKP.

—WXPX XITMKQN

HINTS (SEE PAGE 124): 29, 18
ANSWER ON PAGE 129

WHEN THINGS CLICK

IPH UHHIWQN KR IDK JHVMKQFTWIWHM WM TWXH

IPH SKQIFSI KR IDK SPHUWSFT MCGMIFQSHM: WR

IPHVH WM FQE VHFSIWKQ, GKIP FVH IVFQMRKVUHL.

—SFVT NCMIFB OCQN

HINTS (SEE PAGE 124): 33, 24
ANSWER ON PAGE 129

THINK ABOUT THE INSCRUTABLE

PBT OXUP WTQFPVSFI TGJTHVTKMT RT MQK BQNT

VU PBT OCUPTHVXFU. VP VU PBT SFKEQOTKPQI

TOXPVXK PBQP UPQKEU QP PBT MHQEIT XS PHFT

QHP QKE PHFT UMVTKMT.

—QIWTHP TVKUPTVK

HINTS (SEE PAGE 124): 10, 17
ANSWER ON PAGE 130

RIMSHOT, PLEASE

Q EVSW YGHS V GWVJ OHCLM TWQLMFHGMHHP.

HTEW V LCA XCJJWP V NTQYW HT SW. Q NTWI MW

IVKT'O V XGHYWKKQHTVJ, OMW NTQYW MVP

FCOOWG HT QO.

—GHPTWA PVTLWGYQWJP

HINTS (SEE PAGE 124): 12, 27
ANSWER ON PAGE 130

NO LAUGHING MATTER

MHOKI PG V GJIPKHG DMPWA. P QPUJ DK DMPWU

KT PD VG KWJ KT KHI AIJVDJGD JVIQPJGD WVDHIVQ

IJGKHISJG, LMPSM OHGD YJ EIJGJIXJN VD

VQQ SKGDG.

—CVOJG DMHIYJI

HINTS (SEE PAGE 124): 2, 23
ANSWER ON PAGE 130

SHOW ME THE MONEY!

```
R W P K H I A E G U I L D E R
U I E N A M N Y D Y F D N A R
P L R A I L U A I R C E U R O
E A I R P E E R H U U K O R Y
E Z N A U M H K T G G O P D K
Q T G L R P H K E L F U G I O
J E G L T I S Y W H U A O R R
U U I O N R U H T A S G E H U
O Q T D D A I A I K C W N A N
N E Y N N I L C Z L R H E M A
E S R P I A N N W N L O A N C
R C U I E R K A L A A I N Q A
J U B I A S O R R K R W N E T
X D L H Y L O F G F U D K G A
T O E B O L I V I A N O Y H P
```

AFGHANI (Afghanistan)

BOLIVIANO (Bolivia)

DINAR (Algeria)

DIRHAM (UAE)

DOLLAR (USA)

ESCUDO (Cape Verde)

EURO (European Union)

FORINT (Hungary)

FRANC (Switzerland)

GOURDE (Haiti)

GUILDER (Curacao)

KORUNA (Czech Republic)

KRONE (Denmark)

KWACHA (Zambia)

KWANZA (Angola)

LEK (Albania)

LEMPIRA (Honduras)

NAKFA (Eritrea)

NEW SHEKEL (Israel)

NGULTRUM (Bhutan)

OUGUIYA (Mauritania)

PATACA (Macau)

PESO (Mexico)

POUND (United Kingdom)

QUETZAL (Guatemala)

RAND (South Africa)

RIAL (Iran)

RINGGIT (Malaysia)

RUBLE (Russia)

RUPEE (India)

RUPIAH (Indonesia)

SHILLING (Tanzania)

YEN (Japan)

YUAN (China)

ANSWER ON PAGE 130

SUMMER OLYMPICS

```
G X B O X I N G K G B A O T G S P
G N I C N E F G O K S H H R N C S
M O F L G N I L C Y C A U I I I U
H H D N L I O L X S R N I P M T R
Z T I G R N L Z I C H D P L M S F
C A S T G A B N H S I B O E I A I
K R C J B R N E U F G A L J W N N
Q A U E O E R S R O H L E U S M G
Y M S W T Y Q U D D J L V M B Y N
P A I Z R O F U L U U V A P P G I
B N S Y A L E R E J M B U F R G L
G L G S M O L U S S P C L L I Z E
T F S H O O T I N G T Z T O R L V
B A D M I N T O N D G R U G B Y A
T U P T O H S O G N I V I D O D J
D E C A T H L O N J X E D A S H T
U K A R A T E N O L H T A T N E P
```

ARCHERY	EQUESTRIAN	KARATE	SHOOTING
BADMINTON	FENCING	LONG JUMP	SHOTPUT
BASEBALL	GOLF	MARATHON	SURFING
BOXING	GYMNASTICS	PENTATHLON	SWIMMING
CYCLING	HANDBALL	POLE VAULT	TENNIS
DASH	HIGH JUMP	RELAYS	TRIPLE JUMP
DECATHLON	HURDLES	ROWING	
DISCUS	JAVELIN	RUGBY	ANSWER ON PAGE 130
DIVING	JUDO	SAILING	

VEGGIES

```
O R A T C N E T H C A N I P S
D F Z S A R K O H G T N Y Z K
R E U R R O K M G A Q R P C E
A N C E R C R A R R E N A A E
H N C P O J E T E L A K R B L
C E H P T H B O E I P X S B V
B L I E A S M C N C E K N A S
R P N P T A U U S H A U I G E
O S I O O U C I S Y S T P E V
C E J N P Q U E L H A I T M I
C V I I R S C B S S R M D N H
O I C O E U E O D A C O V A C
L L A N L E T T U C E F O U R
I O M R T A L U G U R A U M Q
B R A B U H R F S N A E B R A
```

ARUGULA	CORN	OKRA	SQUASH
AVOCADO	CUCUMBER	OLIVES	TARO
BEANS	FENNEL	ONION	TOMATO
BEET	GARLIC	PARSNIP	TURNIP
BROCCOLI	GREENS	PEAS	YAM
CABBAGE	JICAMA	PEPPERS	ZUCCHINI
CARROT	KALE	POTATO	
CELERY	LEEK	RADISH	ANSWER ON PAGE 130
CHARD	LETTUCE	RHUBARB	
CHIVES	MUSHROOM	SPINACH	

FAMOUS GOLFERS

```
T R A W E T S H O G A N A E S
S N I C K L A U S J O N E S D
N I V A P R I B I P X L K O O
E N P A M M Z O A Y I M W R O
D I I O E X C R Y K I E A B W
E W U T V E Y O S D P R T I G
K R H A G E N S D A E E S H Z
E I E D E P N L Y Y R F O W Q
R C T Y I G E T A O T A N K D
R A I O A C A L U K R T Z G A
E S K L O U P R G R U L O E E
M P L F U R Y K C G I C I C N
L E F E K T R E V I N O H C S
A R R R E L L I M U A O N A M
P R E L W O F V A R D O N C R
```

ARMOUR, Tommy	**HOGAN, Ben**	**OUIMET, Francis**	**STEWART, Payne**
BOROS, Julius	**IRWIN, Hale**	**PALMER, Arnold**	**TREVINO, Lee**
CASPER, Billy	**JONES, Bobby**	**PAVIN, Corey**	**VARDON, Harry**
DAY, Jason	**KITE, Tom**	**PLAYER, Gary**	**VENTURI, Ken**
ELS, Ernie	**KOEPKA, Brooks**	**ROSE, Justin**	**WATSON, Tom**
FLOYD, Ray	**KUCHAR, Matt**	**SARAZEN, Gene**	**WOODS, Tiger**
FOWLER, Rickie	**MCILROY, Rory**	**SCOTT, Adam**	
FURYK, Jim	**MIDDLECOFF, Cary**	**SNEAD, Sam**	**ANSWER ON PAGE 130**
GARCÍA, Sergio	**MILLER, Johnny**	**SNEDEKER, Brandt**	
HAGEN, Walter	**NICKLAUS, Jack**	**SPIETH, Jordan**	

POPULAR STREET NAMES

```
N M S G H N O T G N I H S A W
O G L B R I C H U R C H Y O Y
S N C E R E L O O S R E L Q G
K I E K U O E L A Z L L G O T
C R D R F R A N K L I N A G U
A P A A N L V D A W I L S O N
J S R P I N E V W A L N U T T
N O S R E F F E J A L S G Y S
D A O R L I A R I P Y D C R E
E C U R P S N B M C U O E O H
L I N C O L N M A I N O N K C
A S U N S E T M P R M W T C D
K N O S N H O J L S I G E I T
E C H E R R Y M E C L O R H E
T F O R E S T D N A L D O O W
```

BROADWAY	GREEN	MILL	WALNUT
CEDAR	HICKORY	OAK	WASHINGTON
CENTER	HILL	PARK	WILLOW
CHERRY	JACKSON	PINE	WILSON
CHESTNUT	JEFFERSON	RAILROAD	WOODLAND
CHURCH	JOHNSON	SPRING	
DOGWOOD	LAKE	SPRUCE	ANSWER ON PAGE 130
ELM	LINCOLN	SUNSET	
FOREST	MAIN	SYCAMORE	
FRANKLIN	MAPLE	VALLEY	

LET ME "RE" WORD THAT

```
L R R E C U R M E E D E R P R
A E E A T R E C E I V E R E E
R I E C W N H C A E R E M S P
E E R G I R E L I G I O U S U
E R V E U T Z S R V T S B X T
L L E E F F A M E E U N T R A
F E R A R L E L G R A V E F B
M V E W D E E R E M P M S R L
L E L S U F N C E G I E E E E
A R I C Q I K T T T R N R S L
E S S U U O R T E R E Q R O A
R E H V N C N A T W L L H R G
R C I T S I L A E R A J P T E
L L A C E R E P E A T N A E R
Y L E R D M T N A V E L E R R
```

REACH
READ
REALISTIC
REALM
REAM
RECALL
RECEIVER
RECITAL
RECKON
RECUR

REDEEM
REEL
REF
REFLECT
REFUGEE
REGAL
REIN
RELATE
RELEVANT
RELIGIOUS

RELISH
RELY
REMIT
REMOTE
RENT
REPEAT
REPLETE
REPRESENT
REPUTABLE
RESCUE

RESET
RESORT
RETRO
REVEL
REVERENT

ANSWER ON PAGE 130

CALCUDOKU 8

ANSWER ON PAGE 131

15+		4	5+		4+
6		1	12+		
3+	4+	7+	7+		6
				10+	
4	5	3	8+		7+
5+		6		4	

CALCUDOKU 9

ANSWER ON PAGE 131

5	11+	1	7+		2
6+		6	8+	6+	
		6+		10+	6
9+			3+		
5+		8+		6	9+
2	4		6		

CALCUDOKU 10

ANSWER ON PAGE 131

2	4	9+		7+	1
11+	4+		8+		9+
	7+			1	
1	7+		9+	15+	
13+	2	7+		4	
				5+	

CALCUDOKU 11

ANSWER ON PAGE 131

3-	7+	1	1-		3
		3:	24×		10×
4	3-		0-		
4-		3			2:
	4	5	12+	18×	
2:					6

CALCUDOKU 12

ANSWER ON PAGE 131

6×		1-		0-	
6	4	2	3	4×	
10×		5-			2:
20×		15×	4	6×	
	1		4-		40×
2:		1			

CALCUDOKU 13

ANSWER ON PAGE 131

0-		2-	2-	5	15×
	2-			1	
1-		1	2	3	10+
	2-		6×		
5+		30×		6	2
6×			9+		1

SUDOKU 8

ANSWER ON PAGE 131

				3				
	3	4	5			8		
8		7						1
	8	2			3	7	5	
			4		9			
	4	3	8			9	2	
7						4		9
		1			5	2	8	
				9				

SUDOKU 9

ANSWER ON PAGE 131

2			3				5	
5		8	7				2	9
				1				
		7						5
	5	9				1	8	
8						9		
				5				
6	3				8	7		2
	4				7			8

SUDOKU 10

ANSWER ON PAGE 131

9						8		
		7	5		8			2
		1			2		9	
8		3			6			
	4	6				7	3	
			1			4		6
	9		3			1		
1			2		5	9		
		4						7

SUDOKU 11

ANSWER ON PAGE 132

2	6			9	3			
					2		5	
7					6			9
						1	2	
	3		2		5		4	
	2	4						
1			5					7
	7		6					
			3	7			9	6

SUDOKU 12

ANSWER ON PAGE 132

		6			8	9		
4	5		3	9				8
			5	6			4	
						2	1	
5			6		2			9
	9	3						
	3			7	4			
6				8	3		9	1
		7	1			4		

SUDOKU 13

ANSWER ON PAGE 132

		6		2	8			4
				5			1	6
8			4			7		2
	8					9		
4								7
		3					8	
3		8			4			9
7	6			3				
1			2	7		5		

GOLF TOURNAMENT

Four talented golfers competed in a tournament round. We missed the action, but we have partial reports on scores and know that each player exhibited strength in a specific area of his game and carried some distinctive equipment in his golf bag (clubs fitted with titanium shafts, special hybrid woods, a 60° wedge, or a putter with an oversized mallet head). So, with the helpful clues set out below, let's figure out who is whom and who shot the lowest score.

1. The four contestants were Gary, the player who hit the longest drives, the one who used hybrids, and the one who scored lowest.

2. Between the longest driver and the player who shot 72, one was Gary and the other used the oversized putter.

3. Grant scored higher than Greg but lower than Gordon (who didn't shoot 71). The best chipper shot 75.

4. The player with titanium-shafted clubs was either Gary or Grant; Gary is not the best putter among the four.

ANSWER ON PAGE 132

	LONG DRIVER	BEST WITH IRONS	CHIPPING CHAMP	TOPS IN PUTTING	TITANIUM SHAFTS	HYBRID CLUBS	60° WEDGE	OVERSIZED PUTTER	69	71	72	75
GARY												
GORDON												
GRANT												
GREG												
69												
71												
72												
75												
TITANIUM SHAFTS												
HYBRID CLUBS												
60° WEDGE												
OVERSIZED PUTTER												

BACKYARD GARDEN PLANS

Down on Shady Lane, four homeowners with sunny backyards are preparing their gardens for the growing season. All will grow flowers and vegetables—and have favorites in each category—but each has a different-sized garden plot. See if you can figure out, based on the clues, what is the favorite flower and vegetable for each gardener and how big her garden is.

1. Pam's favorite vegetable to grow is cucumbers, but she doesn't have the largest garden; neither does the gardener who wants to plant marigolds nor the woman who is a fan of tomatoes.

2. Portia has a larger garden than Pat but a smaller one than Pam.

3. Neither the person with the smallest garden plot nor the begonia fancier wants to grow eggplants.

4. One of those with a garden plot 25 sq. ft. larger than another favors squash.

5. Portia's garden, which won't have squash, is not next to the largest.

6. The prime flower in Pat's garden will be daylilies, while neither Pam nor Portia plans to plant begonias, and Pam is skipping marigolds, too.

ANSWER ON PAGE 132

	BEGONIAS	DAYLILIES	HYDRANGEAS	MARIGOLDS	CUCUMBERS	TOMATOES	EGGPLANTS	SQUASH	100 SQ. FT.	125 SQ. FT.	140 SQ. FT.	150 SQ. FT.
PAM PEATMOSS												
PAT PLANTER												
PENNY PRUNER												
PORTIA PULLWEEDS												
100 SQ. FT.												
125 SQ. FT.												
140 SQ. FT.												
150 SQ. FT.												
CUCUMBERS												
TOMATOES												
EGGPLANTS												
SQUASH												

A DAY AT THE BEACH

Two women and two men are driving to the beach for the day and, as each gets in the car, they throw in something to eat or drink, something to play with, and something to read while they are at the beach. Although it's all a jumble in the back of the car, try to sort out who brought what based on the clues you're given.

1. One of the two men brought the Frisbee, but neither brought the ice cream treats.

2. The person who brought the cookies, who wasn't Skip, also brought a badminton set.

3. Samantha thanked the person who brought the cookies for choosing her favorite, and Sandi, who hadn't gotten the cookies for the group, said she was glad two others had brought cards and the day's newspaper.

4. Skip was not the one who brought the sodas or the newspaper.

5. The cards and the ice cream treats were contributed by different people, and neither brought the puzzle book with them.

6. Samantha brought the novel along for beach reading.

ANSWER ON PAGE 132

	CHIPS	COOKIES	ICE CREAM TREATS	SODA	BADMINTON SET	BEACH BALL	CARDS	FRISBEE	MAGAZINE	NEWSPAPER	NOVEL	PUZZLE BOOK
SAMANTHA												
SANDI												
SKIP												
STU												
MAGAZINE												
NEWSPAPER												
NOVEL												
PUZZLE BOOK												
BADMINTON SET												
BEACH BALL												
CARDS												
FRISBEE												

STOCKING THE SHELVES

Greta Grocer just got some canned vegetables in from her supplier, so she is ready to restock her shelves. The canned goods come in a variety of vegetables, can sizes, and the number of cans of each veggie. Let's see if we can figure out, with the help of the clues, what will be there on the shelves when the store opens tomorrow morning.

1. Greta got more cans of sweet corn than carrots, but less than the cans of peas received.

2. The cans of carrots are twice as large as the cans of another veggie.

3. Neither the sweet corn nor the carrots is a Happy Eats product, but one of them came in an even number of cans.

4. There are twice the number of cans of sweet corn as there are cans of carrots.

5. Neither the peas nor the store brand products come in 12 oz. cans.

6. The green beans are from Super Fresh, but the sweet corn is not a Quick Veggies brand.

7. The sweet corn didn't come in 8 oz. or 24 oz. cans, and the 15 cans of a veggie are not 12 oz. cans.

ANSWER ON PAGE 132

	HAPPY EATS	QUICK VEGGIES	STORE BRAND	SUPER FRESH	8 OZ.	12 OZ.	16 OZ.	24 OZ.	5 CANS	7 CANS	10 CANS	15 CANS
CARROTS												
GREEN BEANS												
PEAS												
SWEET CORN												
5 CANS												
7 CANS												
10 CANS												
15 CANS												
8 OZ.												
12 OZ.												
16 OZ.												
24 OZ.												

EASTER BASKETS

Two families with small children celebrate Easter together by giving their kids baskets full of candy and a dyed Easter egg. The kids compare notes about their baskets—what color egg was in their basket, how many chocolate drops they got, and which is their favorite other candy in the basket. If we use the clues below, we can figure out what each kid had in their Easter basket before its contents disappear.

1. Jelly beans are not the favorite of the kids who got blue and green eggs; the child with the most chocolate drops didn't get a pink egg.

2. Either Erin or Brian is a real fan of gummies; the other got more chocolate drops than any other child.

3. The child whose basket contains 8 chocolate drops didn't get a pink or green egg; the child with the fewest chocolate drops doesn't prefer gummies over other candy.

4. Tommie got fewer chocolate drops than Emma, who didn't get 10. Erin liked her pink Easter egg.

5. The child with the fewest chocolate drops didn't put candy corn or jelly beans at the top of the candy list.

6. Neither Baker kid got a green egg.

7. Emma, who doesn't like candy corn, didn't get a blue egg.

ANSWER ON PAGE 132

	BLUE-DYED EGG	GREEN-DYED EGG	PINK-DYED EGG	YELLOW-DYED EGG	7 CHOC. DROPS	8 CHOC. DROPS	10 CHOC. DROPS	12 CHOC. DROPS	CANDY CORN	GUMMIES	JELLY BEANS	MARSHMALLOWS
ERIN JONES												
TOMMY JONES												
EMMA BAKER												
BRIAN BAKER												
CANDY CORN												
GUMMIES												
JELLY BEANS												
MARSHMALLOWS												
7 CHOC. DROPS												
8 CHOC. DROPS												
10 CHOC. DROPS												
12 CHOC. DROPS												

PUTTING IN THE CROPS

Simon Farmer taught his four children how to farm, and all went into the business. This year, since Simon is getting up in years, he asked each of the kids to farm one of his four fields for him, which they have agreed to do. By following the clues below, we can get a snapshot of what the Farmer farm is going to look like this year as the kids go forward with their plans to help out their dad.

1. Sam will be working his dad's largest field, but he is not planting rice or corn on it and won't be applying chemicals with crop-dusting.

2. Scott will not be farming the 80-acre tract or using drip irrigation, and Sandra won't be planting corn.

3. Forward contracting won't be used to market either the corn crop or the crop grown on the 40-acre tract.

4. Sam is not using drip irrigation on his crop or planting biotech-engineered seeds; Sandra is not growing wheat or rice.

5. Scott is not working the 60-acre plot, and Sean is not planning on using drip irrigation or crop-dusting.

6. One of the three boys is working the 80-acre tract.

ANSWER ON PAGE 132

	40 ACRES	60 ACRES	80 ACRES	120 ACRES	CORN	RICE	SOYBEANS	WHEAT	BIOTECH SEEDS	CROP DUSTER	DRIP IRRIGATION	FORWARD CONTRACT
SAM												
SANDRA												
SCOTT												
SEAN												
BIOTECH SEEDS												
CROP DUSTER												
DRIP IRRIGATION												
FORWARD CONTRACT												
CORN												
RICE												
SOYBEANS												
WHEAT												

BASEBALL FRONT OFFICE ANALYSIS

The High City Hurricanes, one of America's top baseball franchises, is looking to sign a slugger to fill a gap in their lineup. Their preliminary front office analysis has spotlighted four available players who could provide the hitting punch they are looking for. Each player's stats and salary from last season aren't specified in the puzzle grid below, but, by following the clues, maybe you can deduce that information for each one and make your own choice on whom they should hire.

1. One of the two players who hit over .310 last year also hit 37 home runs.

2. Sid didn't have the lowest batting average or home run total, but his batting average was lower than Harry's.

3. Of the two players who hit fewer than 40 home runs, one had a .309 batting average and the other got paid the most.

4. Even though neither Sal nor Sid was the lowest paid last year, one of them only hit .280.

5. Don didn't get paid $8.3 million, nor did he hit 41 home runs or bat .332.

6. The player who hit the most home runs didn't have a .332 batting average, and Harry didn't hit .309.

7. Harry got paid $10 million last year.

8. Sid didn't make $7.3 million or hit 41 home runs last year.

ANSWER ON PAGE 132

	$6 MILLION	$7.3 MILLION	$8.3 MILLION	$10 MILLION	32 HOME RUNS	37 HOME RUNS	41 HOME RUNS	50 HOME RUNS	.280 BAT. AV.	.309 BAT. AV.	.315 BAT. AV.	.332 BAT. AV.
DON DINGER												
HARRY HITTER												
SAL SMASHER												
SID SLUGGER												
.280 BAT. AV.												
.309 BAT. AV.												
.315 BAT. AV.												
.332 BAT. AV.												
32 HOME RUNS												
37 HOME RUNS												
41 HOME RUNS												
50 HOME RUNS												

4

DIFFICULT PUZZLES

HIGH GRADE

TRIVIA CHALLENGE
Which New York City skyscraper erected in 1931 was the world's tallest building for nearly 40 years?

ANSWER ON PAGE 124

Across

1. "Neato!"
5. Canned product since 1937
9. Struck down, in the Bible
14. Diva Gluck
15. ___ *la Douce*, 1963 film
16. Spud
17. So-so evergreens?
19. Aromatic compound
20. First name in cosmetics
21. Carrier to Tokyo
22. Minute particles
23. Skin: Suffix
25. 19th-cent. French composer
27. Never, during a police officer's walking patrol?
31. *NY Times* columnist
35. Laundry detergent brand
36. "___ never work!"
37. Gently calm (someone)
39. Adhesive
41. Long, long time
43. Up to
44. Clothing
46. Bombard
48. Part of i.e.
49. Ogle
50. Kid's winter coat decorated with Disney or Star Wars characters?
53. Additionally
55. Small batteries
56. Swelling
59. Dracula, at times
61. Around (of dates)
65. Get in shape, as for a fight
66. Unable to pick up on someone's effort to make amends?
68. Like Eric the Red
69. Went by horse
70. Alleviate
71. High grade . . . or a clue to the answers of 17, 27, 50, and 66 Across
72. All even
73. What 56 Down will do at times

Down

1. Bistro
2. Waves: Sp.
3. Leave off
4. Southern border city
5. "Dear" one
6. Introductory statement
7. Augusta's "___ Corner"
8. Indian spice mix
9. Purloin
10. Extinct large mammal with tusks
11. One of four Holy Roman emperors
12. Abound
13. Goofs up
18. Descriptive of 55 Across as compared, say, to flashlight batteries
24. Snitch
26. Cadillac model from 2012 to 2019
27. Katmandu's land
28. Speechify
29. Flavor
30. Skip the big wedding
32. Aquatic mammal
33. Type of broom, or kitchen utensil
34. Atlanta-based airline
38. Forge ahead of
40. Sponge cake, mascarpone, and chocolate confection
42. Plant parasite
45. Space invaders, for short
47. Meadow
51. Capital of Tasmania
52. Parenthetical comments
54. Bowling alley units
56. Europe's highest volcano
57. Let fall
58. Tiger's father, ___ Woods
60. Yours: Fr.
62. Harvest
63. Detective's assignment
64. Several
67. Homer's TV neighbor

ANSWER ON PAGE 133

DIMENSIONS

1	2	3	4		5	6	7	8		9	10	11	12	13
14					15					16				
17			18							19				
20							21	22			23			
24								25		26				
			27			28		29					30	31
32	33	34			35		36			37				
38				39					40			41		
42		43			44						45			
46				47			48		49					
		50							51			52	53	54
55	56			57		58		59						
60			61			62	63							
64						65					66			
67						68					69			

TRY THIS!

Ever feel defeated by a puzzle? Don't give up and check the answer. Simply put it down and return later.

Across

1. Canaanite deity
5. Good name for a Dalmatian
9. *All That Jazz* director
14. Utah ski area
15. Kudzu, for one
16. Treated soil to reduce acidity
17. *Wee pedal digit
19. Overjoy
20. Alexandra Feodorovna was the last one
21. Blend, combine
23. PC linkup initials
24. Powerful
25. Streamlet
27. Wall Street pessimist
29. Money-back sales lures
32. "I Got You ____"
35. Glittery fabric
37. France's longest river
38. *Wheel of Fortune* buy
39. Considerable, substantial [or a "punny" way to describe the answers to the four starred (*) clues]
41. Hr. part
42. *Casablanca* star, familiarly
44. Fencer's blade
45. Exploit
46. Dumps
48. Okeechobee, for one
50. Genesis grandson
51. Tunic worn by men in Near East countries
55. Near Eastern honorific
57. R.N.'s forte
59. Sicily's capital
60. Bullion unit
62. *Companies with lots of assets, in investors' slang
64. Purple shade
65. Double-reed instrument
66. Mosaic piece
67. Take an oath
68. Lacunae
69. Musher's transport

Down

1. Latvians, e.g.
2. Most-wanted invitees
3. ___ of roses (perfume ingredient)
4. Pennsylvania town that Arnold Palmer called home
5. Manipulator of others, so named for a character in du Maurier's *Trilby*
6. Hummus holder
7. Lennon's love
8. Abound
9. Supple, pliable
10. Black gold
11. *Two-bit
12. ___ good example
13. Hebrew for "delight"
18. Long narrow strip
22. Anger
26. Neighbor of a Vietnamese
28. Demolishes
29. Defy authority
30. Buffalo's lake
31. Dispatch
32. Hindu "Sir"
33. Soon, to a bard
34. *Opposite of 11 Down
36. Navigator's need
39. Marine mammal seen off the West Coast
40. These occur if there are holes in the dike
43. Charged particle
45. Shortcomings
47. High-speed Internet inits.
49. Trendy green
52. Lag behind
53. Plentiful
54. Beat (out) just barely
55. Goals
56. Bite like a beaver
58. Blockage
59. Support, with "up"
61. Egg cells
63. Lawyers' org.

ANSWER ON PAGE 133

BIG BLUE MARBLE

Across

1. Tibetan priest
5. Character in *A Midsummer Night's Dream*
11. Twitch
14. Mysterious craft
15. Typos
16. Beluga yield
17. Gaia
19. Goal
20. Call's opposite, in the options market
21. At the summit of
22. Rent agreement
24. Swamp
26. Measures
28. Places where you can see the sky inside
33. _____ days (now)
36. African antelope
37. Tribe in Manitoba
38. 5th-century warrior
39. Its capital is Mogadishu
42. Key pt. of Gr. Brit.
43. Arm bone
45. Mechanical routine
46. Small songbird
48. One who's traveled widely
51. World-weary
52. Bring to a boil?
56. Taxpayer on April 15
58. North Atlantic shipping hazard, for short
60. Mafia boss
61. ___ Baba
62. Annual autumn event . . . or a possible description of the answers to 17, 28, and 48 Across as a group
66. Fall from grace
67. Animated movie franchise
68. Lima's land
69. Create a Facebook link to
70. Congregate
71. 30 Down, for one

ANSWER ON PAGE 133

Down

1. Coal or sugar units
2. Run ___ of (violate)
3. "All for one and one for all," e.g.
4. Baseball bat wood
5. Big _____ (large cannon)
6. Creme cookie
7. Ensnare
8. Black gunk
9. NY Giants great
10. Great 19th-cent. composer-conductor
11. Dated name for CFO
12. Charged particles
13. Grant
18. Outstanding golf feats
23. ___ fail (spectacularly embarrassing mistake)
25. Increases
26. Sharp-pointed instrument
27. Metered vehicle
29. "Stop!"
30. See 71 Across
31. Word on a wall, in the Bible
32. Utah lily
33. Hoodlum
34. Ship's body
35. Lending dignity to
40. Table scraps
41. Get even for
44. Competent
47. Like some vbs.
49. Small pincered insect
50. Less wordy
53. "Farewell, mon ami"
54. Plural noun commonly used with "party" or "movie"
55. Follow
56. Ramadan observance
57. Hip bones
58. Said three times, comparable to "yada, yada, yada"
59. (With "out") barely beat
63. Edible S.A. tuber
64. Emeritus: Abbr.
65. Engine speed initials

RIVALRIES

TRIVIA CHALLENGE
Which continent, Asia or Africa, had more countries in 2019?

ANSWER ON PAGE 124

Across

1. "___ boy!"
5. Reveals
10. Actress Sorvino
14. Encircle, surround
15. Very, in music
16. Yemeni port
17. Longtime professional sport rivalry
20. Bard's "before"
21. Awkward-sounding word meaning "inappropriate"
22. Musical Yoko
23. The tympanic membrane
25. European primrose
29. Sleep state, initially
30. Laze
31. "The loneliest number"
32. Fabric-dyeing technique
35. Get better
36. Curved molding
37. Longtime college sport rivalry
40. Nile bird
41. "I'm working ___!"
42. Versifiers
43. Fam. member
44. Plagues
45. Don't just seem
46. _____ Cinema (film co. that produced *The Lord of the Rings*)
48. Does a daily dental chore
52. Writer Fleming
53. They might be pitched
55. Lawyers' org.
56. Longtime professional sport rivalry
60. Shoppe sign word
61. Clangor
62. European capital
63. Disarray
64. Concluded
65. Actress Cannon

Down

1. Be in accord
2. Coronet
3. Judge, or German city
4. Say further
5. 19th-cent. American showman
6. Indian state
7. Invitation letters
8. Locale for the two teams in 56 Across
9. [not my error]
10. Water conduits
11. True believer
12. Gridiron official, for short
13. Opposite of a ques.
18. Epiphany exclamation
19. Bay
24. Insignificant bits
26. Earthen pot
27. Lifeless
28. Hammer parts
30. Jeans
32. Wee child, to a Scot
33. *Who's Afraid of Virginia Woolf?* author
34. They make planes go faster
35. Sycophantic followers
36. Orchestra section
38. Apollo destination
39. Revolted
44. Sup
45. Hitchcock or Tennyson
47. Michigan and Ontario
48. *All That Jazz* director
49. Impudent
50. African virus
51. Part of WASP
54. *The Metamorphosis* author
56. ___ Kippur
57. Bass, e.g.
58. Toronto-to-Ottawa dir.
59. Pentagon org.

ANSWER ON PAGE 133

HINT, HINT

TRY THIS!
Jump out of your comfort zone, by moving on to puzzles
that are not as easy for you to do.

THE ULTIMATE **BRAIN HEALTH PUZZLE BOOK** FOR ADULTS

Across

1. Type of code or rug
5. And others, for short
9. Cass and Michelle of the singing quartet
14. Building near a silo
15. Ploy
16. Be theatrical
17. African gazelle
19. High-hatter
20. Crafted sound
21. Spanish rice dish
22. Texas Hold'em declaration
25. World's longest river
27. Seasoned sailor
28. "Oh, woe!"
29. For's opposite
31. Toronto basketballer
33. Quadrennial occurrence
37. African antelope
38. Romanian currency unit
40. Chain letters?
41. Pub brew
42. Unusual first name of the protagonist in the first TV Western series
45. Professional reviewer
47. Biblical sea
49. Cozy home
50. ___ gin fizz
53. Neural transmitter
54. Slowly, on a score
55. Boat's steering bar
57. More crass
59. Birch relative
60. Get a car going when the battery is dead . . . or a hint to the beginnings of the answers to 17, 33, and 42 Across
64. Grace word
65. Balm ingredient
66. Colored eye part
67. Have a feeling
68. Geeky sort
69. Perched on

Down

1. Stomach muscles, briefly
2. Grammy category
3. Make a mistake
4. One who believes that things have souls
5. Work units
6. Leisurely river sport activity
7. Opposite of gregarious
8. Albanian currency unit
9. ___ Verde National Park
10. Official pardon
11. Long green
12. Wake Island, e.g.
13. Assail
18. Sister
21. Act of atonement
22. Inarticulate expression of total frustration
23. Grassy plain, in Argentina
24. Accept eagerly
26. Didn't shoot straight
29. Descriptive of a 66 Across
30. Practice in the ring
32. Cantina cooker
34. Moth-_____
35. Most-wanted invitees
36. Odd-numbered page
39. Windows alternative
43. Perpetually young
44. Drop of liquid
46. Tendency to do nothing
48. Captivate
50. Tries
51. City in northern France
52. Like days of yore
54. ___ *Misérables*
56. Gaelic tongue
58. Raced
60. Calendar abbr.
61. "A jealous mistress": Emerson
62. Brazilian city, familiarly
63. Cooking meas.

ANSWER ON PAGE 133

WHAT'S IN A NAME?

TRIVIA CHALLENGE
Which was invented first, the Toll House chocolate chip cookie or the ice cream cone?

ANSWER ON PAGE 124

Across

1. Besides
5. Deep sleep
9. Crosswise, on deck
14. Medicos
15. Mine finds
16. Harsh Athenian lawgiver, who lent his name to an adjectival 51 Down
17. *Star Trek* speed
18. Trendy berry
19. Computer shortcut
20. Beginning to cry?
21. Edibles named after the British noble said to have invented them
23. Do again
25. Caterpillar competitor
26. Shifts, e.g.
28. On impulse
32. Fragment of a bomb, named after the British general who invented the bomb
35. Sailor's affirmative
36. Medal recipient
39. Triumphant cry
40. Bad day for Caesar
41. A Gershwin
42. Type of sweater, named after the British general who outfitted troops in it
46. African vacation expedition
48. Genre for a Joplin
52. Ladies' companions, briefly
55. Work boot feature
56. Image of something as a solid, featureless, two-dimensional shape, named after an 18th-cent. officer of the French court
60. City near Lake Tahoe
61. Model
62. Get one's ducks in ___
63. Indian bread
64. Closely compacted
65. Prefix with byte or watt
66. Like custard
67. Bridge positions
68. Influence
69. Abound

Down

1. British monarch who abdicated
2. Slip-on shoe
3. Minor knee injury
4. Strong Italian coffee
5. What a drink sits on, if one is careful
6. Killer whale
7. "_____ Bobby McGee," made famous by a Joplin
8. Parenthetical comment
9. Fleet commander
10. Orthodontic devices
11. A pop
12. Pooh's Hundred ____ Wood
13. Lows
22. "As you ___"
24. Blonde shade
27. River that flows from France into Germany
29. Dined on
30. Caustic used to make soap
31. Survey choice
33. Third degree?
34. Depilatory brand
36. Greetings
37. Baseball pitcher's stat
38. Battle of Britain grp.
40. Surfing place
42. Some Louisianans
43. Hokkaido native
44. St. Louis's _____ Arch
45. In the past
47. Shocked
49. Glaciation period
50. Run
51. Name (of something) derived from a person's name, of which there are four examples in this puzzle
53. League members
54. Scatter, spread untidily
56. Fries, maybe
57. Brainstorm
58. Telescope part
59. Forum wear

ANSWER ON PAGE 133

EASY AS ABC

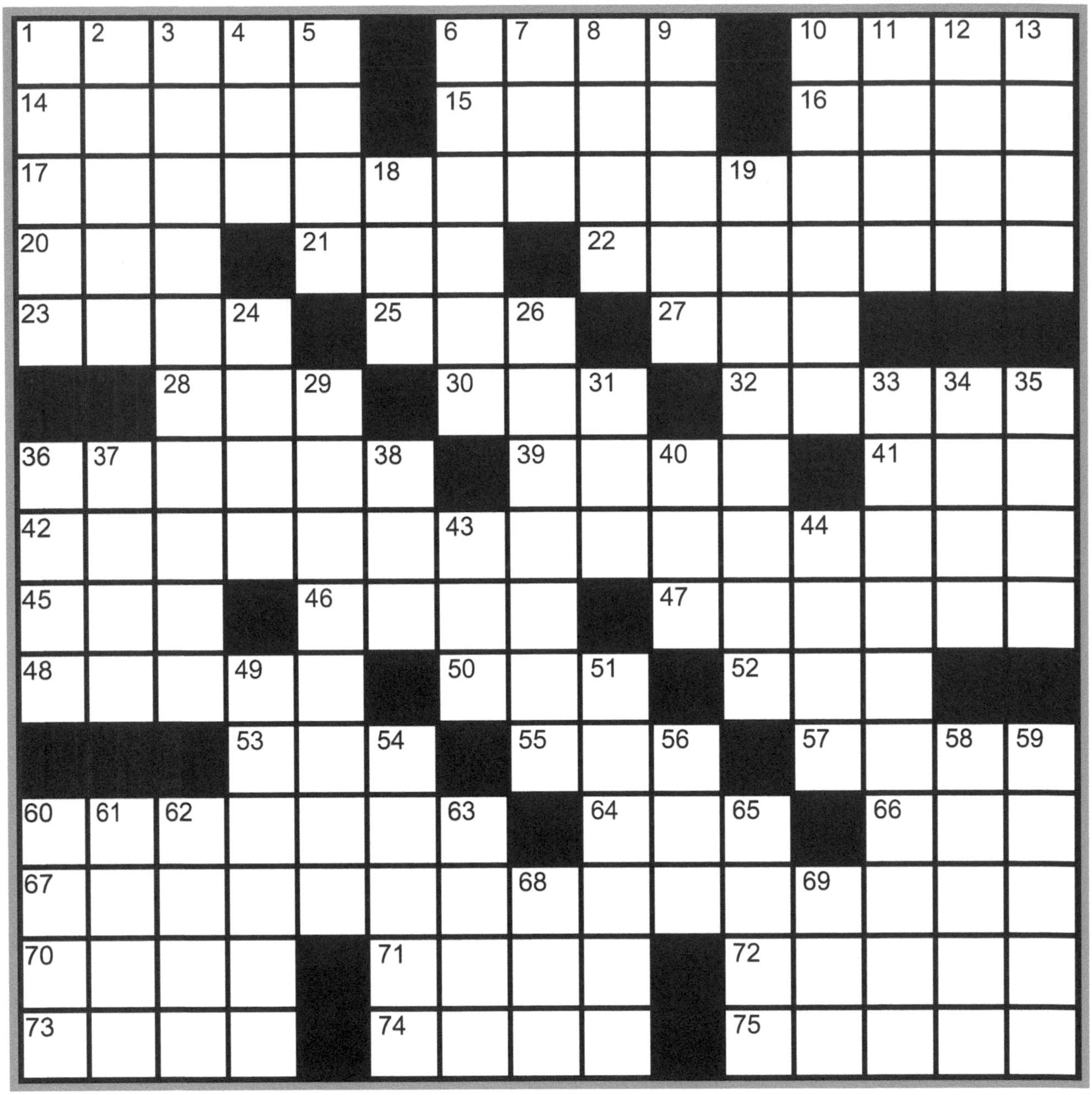

TRY THIS!

How fast can you solve a puzzle? Time yourself. Can you do it faster? Time yourself again.

Across

1. It's a no-no
6. Pioneering video game
10. Moo goo gai pan pans
14. Caribbean game and food fish
15. Asia's ___ Sea
16. Clearasil target
17. Having human characteristics
20. In a ___ (bored)
21. Hail, to Caesar
22. Altruists' opposites
23. Unappetizing food
25. Dadaism founder
27. Clock standard: Abbr.
28. "Spy vs. Spy" magazine
30. Any boat
32. Bridal path
36. Rarely used word meaning to confine (someone) against their will
39. Bakery fixture
41. Arctic diving bird
42. Prominent trait of a firefly
45. Connections
46. Man or Wight
47. Looked after
48. Located, positioned
50. Relatives
52. Plant, as seed
53. Tonic's partner
55. Alumna bio word
57. Speech problem
60. Supervise
64. Perturb
66. Spy org.
67. Person in charge of the cameras and lighting during the making of a movie
70. Diplomacy
71. Hurry
72. Feudal lord, or city in Belgium
73. Bullfight cheers
74. Takes a chair
75. Finished

Down

1. Autocrats of old
2. Invalidate
3. Lowest
4. Cry at a fireworks display
5. Creole vegetable
6. *New York Times*, and others
7. "___ y Plata" (Montana's motto)
8. Appoint
9. Scandinavian Yuletide drink
10. Elk
11. Influential publisher of the *New York Times*
12. Make a sweater, maybe
13. Parts of a min.
18. Egg cells
19. Love stories
24. Newman or Simon
26. Participate in a teleconference
29. Ancient British religious system
31. Night before
33. Like people stuck in a very crowded subway car
34. A founder of *Time* magazine
35. Barely managed, with "out"
36. Bird venerated by ancient Egyptians
37. ___ Cooper
38. Mammal has three
40. Ballpark fig.
43. Kind, sort
44. Organic compound
49. Marsh birds
51. Whinnies
54. Closes in on
56. Drop the ball
58. Military blockade
59. Whittled down
60. Eight: Prefix
61. Medicine bottle
62. Suffix with exist- or persist-
63. Needle case
65. Trendy green
68. Düsseldorf direction
69. Bowling target

ANSWER ON PAGE 133

MOVE ON

MNJNQO RPSO IPL PJI XR ITJR GNKO NK. LTF OPDR ITJR

GOPK LTF STFWI. QTVR XWFJIRUQ PJI PXQFUINKNRQ JT

ITFXK SURHK NJ; MTUARK KORV PQ QTTJ PQ LTF SPJ.

KTVTUUTG NQ P JRG IPL. LTF QOPWW XRANJ NK QRURJRWL

PJI GNKO KTT ONAO P QHNUNK KT XR RJSFVXRURI GNKO

LTFU TWI JTJQRJQR.

—UPWHO GPWIT RVRUQTJ

HINT (SEE PAGE 124): 11
ANSWER ON PAGE 133

TO SUM THINGS UP

XQ JBD UVO GB XOWCGXQJ XC BCW IBAO GUW AWVPBC

IUJ GUW UDHVC AVSW UVP CBG VSUXWLWO VCO CWLWA

IXTT VSUXWLW XGP QDTT MBGWCGXVT, GUVG IBAO IBDTO

NW "HWWGXCYP."

—OVLW NVAAJ

HINT (SEE PAGE 124): 13
ANSWER ON PAGE 133

LIGHTEN UP

FP JBXQWM OXAJTMPD PHPDN MKN WXJL XA FBTOB

FP BKHP AXL MKAOPM KL WPKJL XAOP. KAM FP

JBXQWM OKWW PHPDN LDQLB UKWJP FBTOB FKJ

AXL KOOXRIKATPM SN KL WPKJL XAP WKQVB.

—UDTPMDTOB ATPLGJOBP

HINTS (SEE PAGE 124): 26, 21
ANSWER ON PAGE 133

DEEP THOUGHT

WVQLDH RJ QI VKAVERVIOV, ICDTRIS VPJV. RD RJ

ICD Q MRKVN AQDDVEI CE QI QEEQISVFVID CM

MVQDLEVJ. RD RJ JCFVDTRIS MVPD, Q SPCG CE Q

OCFFLIROQDVN JVIJVN MRIVIVJJ.

—N.T. PQGEVIOV

HINT (SEE PAGE 124): 19
ANSWER ON PAGE 134

A COMMON TRAIT

RJMVF HPNB NBV MBKPMV YVNHVVU MBJUQPUQ KUV'G

XPUF JUF IAKOPUQ NBJN NBVAV PG UK UVVF NK FK

GK, JSXKGN VOVALKUV QVNG YEGL KU NBV IAKKR.

—TKBU DVUUVNB QJSYAJPNB

HINT (SEE PAGE 124): 15
ANSWER ON PAGE 134

KEEP TRYING NEW THINGS

TROXH TCC OUXKX LXTHK, V TI KOVCC VFNGCNXP

VF OUX JHGMXKK GR KXCR-PVKMGNXHL. VO'K

SXOOXH OG XQJCGHX CVRX TFP ITEX IVKOTEXK

OUTF OG JCTL VO KTRX. IVKOTEXK THX JTHO GR

OUX PDXK GFX JTLK RGH T RDCC CVRX.

—KGJUVT CGHXF

HINT (SEE PAGE 124): 34
ANSWER ON PAGE 134

DOG BREEDS

```
I Q C F F I T S A M H E A A V U G
O R H H H C A E S C H N A U Z E R
Z O I U X T C W L J B Q Z T A P E
R B H S I T O X H A T O H X O E A
O R U K H H C Z S J D I X I T D T
B I A Y C S K S S X H E N E H N D
Y T H E L B E W P S W T R Q R U A
M T U W I T R T I P E R G I Z O N
T A A U H E S M T R I R H V A H E
C N L O N A P S Z E E J K B Z Y B
E Y U T I P A R R B R I A R D E U
L N C M E L N Q A E L G A E B R M
D P U G U S I I W H I P P E T G N
O P Y K L I E N M V S E I L L O C
O Y I Z W E L S H C O R G I Z T Z
P A P I L L O N D N U H S H C A D
I N A I T A M L A D B U L L D O G
```

AIREDALE

AKITA

BASSET HOUND

BEAGLE

BORZOI

BOXER

BRIARD

BRITTANY

BULLDOG

CHIHUAHUA

CHOW

COCKER SPANIEL

COLLIE

DACHSHUND

DALMATIAN

GREAT DANE

GREYHOUND

HUSKY

IRISH SETTER

MALTESE

MASTIFF

PAPILLON

POINTER

POODLE

PUG

PUMI

SALUKI

SCHNAUZER

SHAR PEI

SHIH TZU

SPITZ

TERRIER

WELSH CORGI

WHIPPET

ANSWER ON PAGE 134

PRECIOUS STONES

```
L E N I P S A O S C A L C I T E Y
A P N E P H R I T E B A P E A R L
P D C Z E S I O U Q R U T E E A F
I M R S U N S T O N E E A N R M T
S D S U A G A T E M N M I E I S O
L K W O Z Y K L E R E R T R H D U
A F Y P D Y I R A T T I U Y P X R
Z M P A Y A A G R I R B T D P E M
U I E L N L L I C O Y K O I A F A
L L R T D I N I U H Z I D A S E L
I Y L C H E T L T O A O I M I T I
D R Q I O Y F E I E P L R O X I N
R E B M A N S S C R O I E N Y R E
I B K U N Z I T E P T T P D N Y H
J A D E Z T R A U Q A E R H O P V
J A S P E R V A L A R I M A R X K
O B S I D I A N A M M O L I T E Z
```

AGATE	EMERALD	OBSIDIAN	SUNSTONE
AMBER	FLUORITE	ONYX	TOPAZ
AMETHYST	GARNET	OPAL	TOURMALINE
AMETRINE	IOLITE	PEARL	TURQUOISE
AMMOLITE	JADE	PERIDOT	ZIRCON
BERYL	JASPER	PYRITE	ZOISITE
CALCITE	KUNZITE	QUARTZ	
CARNELIAN	KYANITE	RUBY	ANSWER ON PAGE 134
CITRINE	LAPIS LAZULI	SAPPHIRE	
DIAMOND	LARIMAR	SODALITE	
DRUZY	NEPHRITE	SPINEL	

CALIFORNIA TOWNS NAMED AFTER SPANISH SAINTS

```
J T A P S L E A N D R O J M E B J
V O G E I D J O S E S U S A N A Z
E I M D O C S I C N A R F R U R N
N M A R S A E R D N A A O C C B J
E N R O U B M Z B E R S N O L A U
T P I A Z A O A T D A K I S A R A
I Z A G R N U N O M N B D P R A N
A O E T L T E L I I E L R A A Z C
J O I O I M Y R U R Z W A U P K A
O N M S E R I Q O I A E N L N Y P
D C T L W T A G R L S M R A F O I
N A C T E O A G U D D O E T L D S
A R J T J S M M R E I U B B Z C T
N L N A C I N O M A L M A I R I R
R O L E I R B A G K M P A U S W A
E S C U F J L N O M A R Z S V P N
F L E A F A R A K P J A C I N T O
```

san ANDREAS
san ANSELMO
san ARDO
san BERNARDINO
san BRUNO
san CARLOS
san CLEMENTE
san DIEGO
san DIMAS
san FERNANDO
san FRANCISCO

san GABRIEL
san JACINTO
san JOAQUIN
san JOSE
san JUAN BAUTISTA
san JUAN CAPISTRANO
san LEANDRO
san LORENZO
san LUIS OBISPO
san MARCOS
san MARINO

san MARTIN
san MATEO
san MIGUEL
san PABLO
san PEDRO
san RAFAEL
san RAMON
santa ANA
santa BARBARA
santa CLARA
santa CRUZ

santa MARGARITA
santa MARIA
santa MONICA
santa PAULA
santa ROSA
santa SUSANA
santa VENETIA

ANSWER ON PAGE 134

INTERNATIONAL TRAVEL

```
K A T H M A N D U B A N A V A H R
I R G Q Z O P A R I S B G G R Y E
V Q I R P A C I N A A E I N E E Y
M E T H A Q T O R M M I B O M N K
U A N M I L A N E X S J R K O D J
A D D I S A B A B A T I A G R Y A
T T O A C E A H C D E N L N G S V
A A B L G E R A S N R G T O C W I
K S A I W A P E A C D B A H A C K
L M L K A U S J N C A T R D I B L
O A I O L R E C U G M N U X R N A
K N U C N D R R A A E M C N O O E
M I O U O D A I C R R T J U I B R
E A M I L C O A T E V D I P N S T
C M R I A Y U N B Z T B E R L I N
C F L O R E N C E S N E H T A L O
A V M X S E R I A S O N E U B K M
```

ACAPULCO	BUENOS AIRES	KATHMANDU	RABAT
ADDIS ABABA	CAIRO	KOLKATA	REYKJAVIK
AGRA	CANCUN	LIMA	RIO DE JANEIRO
AMSTERDAM	CAPRI	LISBON	ROME
ATHENS	CURACAO	LONDON	SERENGETI
BALI	FLORENCE	MACAU	SYDNEY
BEIJING	GIBRALTAR	MADAGASCAR	TASMANIA
BERLIN	GOA	MECCA	TUNIS
BERMUDA	HANOI	MILAN	VENICE
BERN	HAVANA	MONTREAL	
BIARRITZ	HONG KONG	PARIS	ANSWER ON PAGE 134

ANIMAL GROUP NAMES

```
I Y N O L O C O A L I T I O N T E
P R I D E K O B E W H N X Q B M Y
A D E S C E N T O O D O U R B U C
P B B L J G V H S R P I E A S R A
E A M Z K I O T V P V T R Y O D R
N L N U Z C C C H E S A D R U E I
O T G D H I A U R U S T S R N R P
R Q R G E R T C M S U L C U D D S
D E J O A M I X M K E A O C E Y N
L W D V O G O E C U D X L S R R O
U U A W A P N N T L G E D L K O C
A N B K O T P H I N U M R E W O T
C Y Y E E L B B A U Q S D O P K O
C K Y E V O C G E G M P T Q N E C
E A R R A Y M R A L D P A E L R S
T I R E D N U H T B A T T E R Y K
E C L U T C H Y C N A N I T S B O
```

ARMY of frogs
ARRAY of hedgehogs
BATTERY of barracudas
BEVY of swans
CACKLE of hyenas
CARAVAN of camels
CAULDRON of bats
CETE of badgers
CLOWDER of cats
CLUSTER of spiders
CLUTCH of chickens
COALITION of cheetahs

COLONY of beavers
CONSPIRACY of lemurs
CONVOCATION of eagles
COVEY of quail
DESCENT of woodpeckers
EMBARASSMENT of
  pandas
EXALTATION of larks
GAGGLE of geese
GANG of turkeys
HOST of sparrows
LEAP of leopards

MURDER of crows
MUSTER of storks
OBSTINACY of buffaloes
PANDEMONIUM of
  parrots
POD of dolphins
PRIDE of lions
PROWL of jaguars
QUIVER of cobras
RHUMBA of rattlesnakes
ROOKERY of albatrosses
SCOLD of jays

SCURRY of squirrels
SLEUTH of bears
SOUNDER of boars
SQUABBLE of seagulls
THUNDER of
  hippopotamuses
TOWER of giraffes
TROOP of baboons
WAKE of buzzards

ANSWER ON PAGE 134

US MOUNTAIN PEAKS

```
R I L A N E D S A I N T E L I A S
N A O N R U B K C A L B F T Y K H
O D I Q M A S S I V E O R T O A N
S P I N C H O T R N R N V R Y M I
L H S O I B E A R A G A C E T Q W
I E A A S E Z E K B N S S B L H R
W R J G N O R E L L F N P L E C A
M A H R D F R K X A N J E E L O D
A R D A R C O R I N Y G L W A O K
U D R N A E A R K C N E P H N K A
N O A D V D W E D A R O A I T A E
A U B T R E I G R P W T M T E W P
K R B E A T A W E E S E O N R E S
E A U T H B K A L A T V R E O A G
A Y H O B K K L H K O A G Y R H N
R E T N U H F S M A U N A L O A O
R K A E P N O O R A M S N D O V L
```

BLANCA PEAK co
DENALI ak
GRAND TETON wy
KINGS PEAK ut
LONGS PEAK co
MAROON PEAK co
MAUNA KEA hi
MAUNA LOA hi
mt. ANTERO co
mt. BEAR ak
mt. BLACKBURN ak

mt. BONA ak
mt. COOK ak
mt. DARWIN ca
mt. ELBERT co
mt. EVANS co
mt. FAIRWEATHER ak
mt. FORAKER ak
mt. GABB ca
mt. HARVARD co
mt. HAYES ak
mt. HERARD co

mt. HUBBARD ak
mt. HUNTER ak
mt. KAWEAH ca
mt. KEITH ca
mt. MASSIVE co
mt. MORGAN ca
mt. OSO co
mt. OURAY co
mt. PINCHOT ca
mt. POWELL co
mt. RAINIER wa

mt. SAINT ELIAS ak
mt. SANFORD ak
mt. SHASTA ca
mt. TOM ca
mt. WHITNEY ca
mt. WILSON co
mt. WRANGELL ak
mt. YALE co
WHEELER PEAK nm

ANSWER ON PAGE 134

TYPES OF PASTA

```
A N I L O P I R T O R I S I C V T
Z C H I F F E R I E A T P F I I A
V O A P G T R O F I E U A J R N G
I E I V E E M P Z L S R G E I I L
T G R H A N M A L Y F C H S O T I
T O V M C T N E R A A M E P L A A
O M R D I R E E L Z I E T I E C T
C I R B I C O L E L I N T R I U E
I T I Z F T E T L L I A I A R B L
N I G L O O A L K I L R N L O A L
A F A R R P I L L U S I D I I U E
M R T Z V N X L I I I P R R F F H
K O O L G O I D E N I B R A B L C
S T N U X S A C B P I I U Y M J H
X I I V U K A N E L L I I L G I G
Q N Y F L A S A G N A E N A G A L
E I L I T N U P A C O R Z E T T I
```

ANELLI
BARBINE
BUCATINI
CAPUNTI
CAVATELLI
CHIFFERI
CIRIOLE
CORZETTI
DITALINI
FARFALLE

FILINI
FIORI
FUSILLI
GEMELLI
GIGLI
GOMITI
LAGANE
LASAGNA
LINGUINE
MANICOTTI

MARILLE
MARZIANI
ORZO
PENNE
PILLUS
PIPE
RIGATONI
RISI
ROTINI
SPAGHETTI

SPIRALI
STELLE
TAGLIATELLE
TORCHIO
TRIPOLINA
TROFIE
VERMICELLI
ZITI

ANSWER ON PAGE 134

CALCUDOKU 14

ANSWER ON PAGE 135

1-		3:	4-	100×	
	2:				1-
3+		14+			
	15+			2-	24×
15×	9+		11+		
					1

CALCUDOKU 15

ANSWER ON PAGE 135

2:	3-		6+		2
	2×	14+		13+	
5:				1-	
	16+		1-		2-
90×				13+	
		3			

CALCUDOKU 16

ANSWER ON PAGE 135

2:		1-	3-		4-
7+	5		1-		
		1-		8×	3
17+	3		3:		
		2×		270×	4
	1				

CALCUDOKU 17

ANSWER ON PAGE 135

6×		2-	13+	12+	
4×	10×				
		8×		1:	
5+	1-		2-		
				5:	3:
90×			4		

CALCUDOKU 18

ANSWER ON PAGE 135

30×	2-		40×	1-	
		4:			6+
2:			72×	6	
	7+				9+
144×		30×		5:	
			1		4

CALCUDOKU 19

ANSWER ON PAGE 135

72×	6+		0-		6+
		30×			
10×			12+	12×	
	3-			36×	
2-		6×			8×
	5-		20×		

SUDOKU 14

ANSWER ON PAGE 135

		3				1	7	
2				3	6	4		
		5			4		3	
		2	4					
		7	6		8	3		
					2	5		
	3		1			7		
		9	5	4				3
	7	4				6		

SUDOKU 15

ANSWER ON PAGE 135

	9		3					8
			1				6	5
		6	2				3	
		8			4			
		3				2		
			7			6		
	8				5	9		
6	5			2				
1				9			5	

SUDOKU 16

ANSWER ON PAGE 135

1	7						6	
	6		8	2		7		
		4			5			
			6				5	9
	3					2		
4	5				7			
			1			8		
		1		8	3		7	
	8						3	2

SUDOKU 17

ANSWER ON PAGE 136

					8	9		
			9	1				
9		5			6		3	
3	5		4				7	8
		9				2		
7	6				3		9	4
	7		5			8		1
				3	2			
		6	8					

SUDOKU 18

ANSWER ON PAGE 136

		2				5	9	
			7	8				
8			6	2				
		4		7				9
2		9				1		5
7				1		2		
			5	1				2
			9	7				
	4	1				3		

SUDOKU 19

ANSWER ON PAGE 136

						4		3
		2	1			8	5	
			7	4				
	7			2			4	
8		6				5		9
	5			6			3	
			4	9				
	8	3			2	7		
5		7						

FRIDAY NIGHT POKER GAME

Five people at the condo complex enjoy playing penny ante poker and have a game in the club room every Friday night. They rotate among themselves as to who will be "host" and provide the munchies for the group. Each player has their own favorite version of poker as well. From the clues provided below, can you figure out what each person's favorite poker game and game-night snack are, and who won the most the last time they played?

1. The players for last Friday's game included Pam, the person who generally prefers draw poker, the one who always brings peanuts as host, and the guy who broke even.

2. Perry, who doesn't particularly like Texas Hold'em, came out worse, money-wise, than Phil, but better than Penny.

3. For one of the women players, her snack choice invariably is corn chips, while the other woman enjoys playing stud poker.

4. The player that netted $5.75 last Friday is a big fan of Texas Hold'em. Pam, who avoided losing money last Friday, doesn't like stud poker, while Paul, who generally passes on popcorn, loves to play deuces wild whenever he can.

5. Penny, who didn't come in worst, money-wise, does like pretzels and brings them with her when she hosts. Perry doesn't like popcorn.

ANSWER ON PAGE 136

	DEUCES WILD	DRAW POKER	STUD POKER	HIGH-LOW SPLIT	TEXAS HOLD'EM	CORN CHIPS	PEANUTS	POPCORN	POTATO CHIPS	PRETZELS	- $8.40	- $7.50	BROKE EVEN	+ $5.75	+ $10.15
PAM															
PAUL															
PENNY															
PERRY															
PHIL															
- $8.40															
- $7.50															
BROKE EVEN															
+ $5.75															
+ $10.15															
CORN CHIPS															
PEANUTS															
POPCORN															
POTATO CHIPS															
PRETZELS															

BOND PORTFOLIO

Tonya Trustee, who manages a charitable trust, has taken care to put the trust funds to good use by, among other things, acquiring a diverse portfolio of five corporate income-producing bonds. Using the clues provided here, you can take a look inside that portfolio and see for yourself the strategic balance of the trust's bond holdings based on rating, maturity, and amount held in each bond.

1. Each of the two bonds with a maturity three years longer than that of the bond in the portfolio immediately below it in order of maturity carries a rating of either A-2 or B-2. The portfolio's bond issued by Jones & Smith Industries does not have an A rating or a 7-year maturity.

2. The SudoCo bond is smaller in value than the United Businesses, Inc., bond but more than the Prime Products, LLC, bond, while the Great Ventures, Ltd., bond is not the $3,000,000 bond.

3. One of the bonds has a B-1 rating and a maturity of 5 years, but it is not the $1.5 million asset. Both the Great Ventures and Jones & Smith bonds have values of more than $1,000,000.

4. The United Businesses bond is rated B-2, does not carry a 7-year maturity, and is not the $3,000,000 bond, while the Great Ventures bond is not A-2 rated, doesn't come with a 15-year maturity, and is not the $1.5 million bond.

5. The Prime Products bond is not an A-1 or A-2 rated bond, nor does it have a maturity of 7 or 12 years. The 10-year bond has an A-2 rating.

6. The Great Ventures issuance isn't a $1,250,000 bond, nor is the instrument with a 15-year maturity date.

ANSWER ON PAGE 136

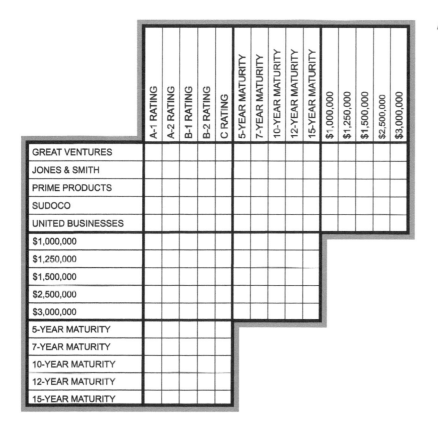

FAVORITE NEWS FEED

Five people are comparing the merits of various news feeds. The clues below reflect some of that discussion, so see if you can figure out from them who prefers which news feed and what is their favorite feature of that feed, and what the consensus of the group is on the strong point for each news feed.

1. Those having the discussion today are Nate, the person who uses the AggreGator news feed, the man whose news feed has what all agree is quality instant news alerts, the person whose favorite news feed feature is its human-interest stories, and Nell.

2. eJournal doesn't carry puzzles, and the consensus is that the NY Sentinel news feed doesn't have good entertainment news, though its fan liked it because of its business updates.

3. Ned doesn't rely on his news feed for human-interest stories, and his feed doesn't have what the group thinks is a strong reporting staff, either. Nils's feed isn't the consensus best for instant news or in-depth analyses, but he prefers it because of its political reports.

4. All agree that NewsHost reporters aren't the best and its feed doesn't provide in-depth analyses. The feeds that Nate and Nora use don't have good in-depth analyses, either.

5. Nora uses eJournal as her news feed, which the group thinks has poor sports coverage compared to other feeds.

6. The person whose news feed everyone considers as having the best instant news doesn't rely on it for business updates or puzzles, and Nate doesn't use his feed to get business updates, either.

7. Neither Nate nor Nora cares that their news feed doesn't have the highest quality reporting. Nate doesn't use the Sentinel's feed or NewsHost.

ANSWER ON PAGE 136

BIRTHDAY LUNCH

It's Cristy's birthday, and four of her friends are celebrating by treating her to lunch at her favorite Chinese restaurant. Everybody orders the luncheon special, which consists of an entrée, a soup, and an appetizer. As you follow the clues provided below, try to determine what the birthday girl and each of her four pals are ordering and enjoying at this birthday feast.

1. Cristy ordered first, then the woman next to her ordered Szechuan pork, followed by the person who ordered seafood soup, then the one who asked for barbecued ribs, and Kayla.

2. Neither Cristy nor Kayla chose the General Tso's shrimp, and Kayla passed on the moo shu beef as well.

3. The appetizers and soup were served together, and the women who got hot and sour soup and pork noodle soup also got fried wontons and steamed dumplings, though not necessarily in that order. Kiki, who avoided the vegetable entrée, the Szechuan chicken, and the seafood soup, was not one of those women.

4. The woman who selected the egg drop soup did not get the barbecued ribs. Carla (sitting next to her) did not order the seafood soup, the pork noodle soup, or the edamame appetizer.

5. Kate chose the vegetable lo mein as her entrée but passed on the barbecued ribs. Cristy, who loves spring rolls, got a double order of them and shared them with the group.

6. The person eating the fried wontons did not have the hot and sour soup.

ANSWER ON PAGE 136

OFFICE SUPPLY STORE RUN

Kayla is the office manager at Rocket Sales, Inc., a small marketing firm. She needs to run to the office supply store to pick up several items and, before heading out, she checked with each of the firm's five sales reps to see what they need while she is there. What she learned is that each of them needs a specific type of writing implement, a small supply item, and a more major acquisition. The clues below provide some information about everyone's requests and should enable you to put together what Kayla's shopping list looks like as she heads out the door.

1. Tiffany told Kayla that she needs lead for her 0.5 mm mechanical pencil. Another of the sales staff wants a new 0.7 mm mechanical pencil, and that person was neither Sid nor Stan, although one of those men needs some red felt-tip pens.

2. One man needs to replace his keyboard and mouse, but he is not also requesting a package of 3x5 cards or paper clips. The man who is asking for paper clips is not the one asking for blue felt-tip pens or black ballpoints. The man who asked Kayla to bring him back some binder clips is one asking for blue felt-tip pens.

3. Sam needs neither black ballpoint pens nor a 0.7 mm mechanical pencil, and the person who wants a ruler is not looking for red felt-tip pens or black ballpoints.

4. As to the bigger things the sales staffers need, neither Sam nor Sid is asking for a reading lamp, and Seth is not looking to replace his chair, but Stan does need a replacement ink cartridge for his printer.

5. Neither Seth nor Sid asked Kayla to get them binder clips or sticky notes, nor did Sid ask her to bring him back red felt-tip pens. Same with the person who wants Kayla to buy sticky notes—he is not looking to get red felt-tip pens.

6. Sam doesn't need to replace his keyboard or chair, and Seth doesn't need a reading lamp.

ANSWER ON PAGE 136

HIGH SCHOOL SPORTS PROGRAMS

It's budget-prep time at Valley View High, and the teachers responsible for supervising the so-called "minor" sports (i.e., not sports like football, basketball, etc.) are getting ready to argue their cases for a share of next year's budget at a special meeting of the finance committee. Each teacher/coach has submitted a budget request based on need and anticipated number of participants for use at the meeting. Using the clues set out below, imagine you are on the finance committee with a very tight budget to allot among five smaller sports and see if you can figure out who is asking for what so you can make your decisions.

1. Mr. Adams, who does not coach the field hockey program, is scheduled to be the first teacher to speak at the meeting, followed by the teacher with the smallest estimated participation in their sport, then the teacher asking for a budget of $7,500, then Ms. Cartwright, and finally Mr. Edison, who coaches the swim team.

2. Mr. Baker, who thinks his sport will draw fewer than 30 participants, is not requesting the smallest budget, but he is not requesting the largest budget, either.

3. The sport seeking the largest budget is not rugby, and its teacher/coach anticipates having more than 25 participants, while the sport whose teacher/coach wants a budget of $6,000 is golf.

4. Neither the golf nor swimming teacher/coach expects the largest number of participants. Actually, Ms. Cartwright, who coaches field hockey, expects her sport to draw more students than the other four sports.

5. Mr. Adams is not seeking a budget of $5,000 or $6,000.

6. Mr. Edison does not peg participation in swimming at 24, nor is he proposing a budget of either $5,000 or $7,200.

ANSWER ON PAGE 136

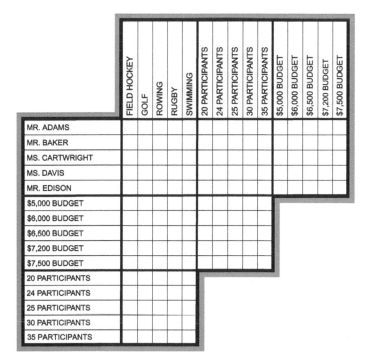

CRYPTOGRAM HINTS

(coded letter = real letter)

1	Z = S	13	B = O	25	C = R
2	Q = L	14	O = N	26	F = W
3	V = I	15	B = H	27	H = O
4	P = A	16	G = R	28	J = N
5	V = O	17	M = C	29	N = U
6	K = E	18	F = T	30	V = M
7	D = H	19	V = E	31	W = R
8	X = I	20	X = P	32	K = N
9	K = N	21	B = H	33	V = R
10	Q = A	22	V = N	34	T = A
11	J = N	23	K = O		
12	P = D	24	K = O		

ANSWERS

Trivia Challenges

Page 20: Venus, Mars

Page 26: Jackie Robinson

Page 58: Elizabeth Cady Stanton

Page 88: Empire State Building

Page 94: Africa

Page 98: ice-cream cone

Warm-Up

SEEING RED

T	I	G	E	R		P	A	C	K		A	F	E	W
A	R	E	N	A		A	L	O	E		E	I	R	E
C	A	N	D	Y	A	P	P	L	E		G	R	A	S
K	N	E	E		N	U	S		P	R	I	E	S	T
			D	A	T	A		G	O	O	S	E		
S	A	P		F	I	N	D	O	U	T		N	A	P
T	R	O	L	L	S		E	N	T	A	N	G	L	E
A	D	I	E	U		R	A	G		T	O	I	L	S
P	O	N	Y	T	A	I	L		B	O	N	N	E	T
H	R	S		T	R	O	T	T	E	R		E	N	S
		E	V	E	R	T		E	L	S	E			
R	E	T	I	R	E		O	N	O		V	E	E	R
E	A	T	S		S	T	R	A	W	B	E	R	R	Y
A	S	I	A		T	H	E	N		A	R	I	S	E
L	E	A	S		S	O	O	T		D	Y	N	E	S

PLEASANT TIMES

Summer afternoon—summer afternoon; to me those have always been the two most beautiful words in the English language.
—Henry James

GEORGE WASHINGTON

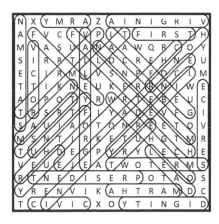

CALCUDOKU 1

1	2	3	4
2	1	4	3
3	4	1	2
4	3	2	1

SUDOKU 1

8	7	3	6	1	9	4	5	2
5	4	1	2	3	7	8	6	9
2	6	9	4	5	8	1	7	3
6	3	5	1	9	2	7	4	8
9	8	7	5	4	3	2	1	6
1	2	4	8	7	6	9	3	5
3	9	8	7	6	1	5	2	4
4	1	6	9	2	5	3	8	7
7	5	2	3	8	4	6	9	1

FUN WITH PUZZLES

Adam, logic puzzles, evenings at home
Bob, word searches, weekends
Carla, sudoku, on travel
Denise, crosswords, on work breaks

Easy Puzzles

OPPOSITES ATTRACT

G	A	Z	E	B	O		L	O	U	T		B	T	U
E	D	I	T	O	R		A	L	S	O		L	O	S
N	I	G	H	T	A	N	D	D	A	Y		I	T	E
E	N	S		S	T	A	Y		O	W	N	E	D	
			E	W	E	R		O	P	T	E	D		
B	A	S	R	A		C	O	M	E	A	N	D	G	O
A	T	H	E	N	A		B	A	P		T	A	L	C
T	A	O		A	N	T	O	N	Y	M		T	A	T
C	R	O	C		I	R	E		S	E	N	E	C	A
H	I	T	O	R	M	I	S	S		N	O	S	E	D
			C	H	E	A	P		A	C	H	T		
S	T	R	O	P		A	R	E	A		C	B	S	
T	E	A		O	P	E	N	A	N	D	S	H	U	T
Y	A	P		R	E	S	T		T	E	R	E	S	A
E	M	S		T	A	P	E		S	N	O	R	T	S

THE FAB FIVE

E	S	T		A	D	M	E	N		H	O	O	T	S
N	O	R		P	R	O	V	E		U	L	N	A	R
A	L	A		R	A	N	E	E		R	A	T	I	O
M	I	C	H	I	G	A	N		R	O	S	A		
O	C	T	A	L		R	E	S	I	N		R	A	T
R	I	O	T		S	C	R	O	D		S	I	D	E
S	T	R	E	T	C	H		L	A	M	P	O	O	N
			F	O	R				B	O	O			
A	R	D	U	O	U	S		P	L	A	I	T	E	D
N	O	E	L		P	E	W	E	E		L	O	S	E
D	E	F		B	L	E	A	R		Y	E	N	T	A
			E	R	I	E		S	U	P	E	R	I	O	R
R	U	N	O	N		L	A	K	E	S		E	N	E
B	A	S	T	E		O	B	E	S	E		S	I	S
G	R	E	A	T		L	I	S	T	S		T	A	T

PUNZAPALOOZA

C	L	I	P		D	U	M	A		A	R	B	O	R
A	O	N	E		E	T	A	S		P	E	R	T	H
P	O	I	N	T	L	E	S	S		P	L	A	T	O
E	N	T	A	I	L		S	E	A		E	V	E	N
			I	L	L		H	E	R	B	I	V	O	R	E
C	P	A		E	C	O		T	A	R	A			
H	A	L	F		O	L	E		L	E	N	N	O	N
U	G	L	I		R	E	T	R	O		C	E	L	L
G	E	Y	S	E	R		C	O	N		E	W	E	R
			H	A	U	L		L	E	S		S	O	B
L	I	V	E	R	P	O	O	L		T	A	P		
O	D	O	R		T	A	O		A	E	R	A	T	E
S	E	L	M	A		T	H	E	C	R	E	P	E	S
E	A	T	A	T		H	E	R	R		N	E	A	P
S	L	A	N	T		E	D	G	E		A	R	M	Y

HE PLAYS A ROLE

M	A	G	I		K	M	A	R	T		W	I	G	S
I	C	O	N		A	C	T	I	I		E	V	E	N
L	E	A	D	I	N	G	M	A	N		B	O	N	O
		I	D	E	A			E	S	C	R	O	W	
L	A	M	A	S		H	I	M	A	L	A	Y	A	S
A	G	I	N		A	N	N	A		E	M	T		
P	A	S	S	U	P		G	R	E	W		O	A	R
S	I	B		S	E	C	R	E	T	E		W	E	E
E	N	E		A	R	I	A		A	D	D	E	R	S
		H	O	G		A	I	N	T		W	R	I	T
C	H	A	P	E	R	O	N	E		B	A	S	E	S
R	E	V	I	S	E			S	U	E	R			
I	L	I	A		G	E	N	T	R	I	F	I	E	S
S	L	O	T		A	L	D	E	N		E	D	G	E
P	O	R	E		L	O	A	D	S		D	O	G	E

STRING QUARTET

F	E	A	S	T		A	S	E	A		H	U	S	H
O	X	B	O	W		P	H	E	W		O	N	T	O
C	E	L	L	O	P	H	A	N	E		S	L	A	Y
I	C	Y		B	A	I	L		S	T	A	L	L	
F	I	D	D	L	E	D	E	E	D	E	E			
C	H	A	R	T	S			D	O	L	L	Y		
A	I	R	Y		B	A	G	E	L		L	O	P	
R	E	B		T	E	E	T	E	R	S		I	V	E
P	S	I		O	W	N	E	R		S	K	E	W	
	T	O	W	E	D		B	I	K	E	R	S		
H	A	R	P	E	R	S	F	E	R	R	Y			
E	M	A	I	L		A	M	O	K		A	L	E	
R	I	T	A		L	U	K	E	W	I	L	S	O	N
S	C	O	T		U	S	E	R		N	A	S	T	Y
H	E	R	E		G	A	R	Y		G	O	T	T	A

"I'M IMPRESSED"

B	O	A	R	D		C	R	E	W		H	A	U	L
I	D	L	E	R		H	E	R	A		O	G	R	E
B	I	G	C	Y	P	R	E	S	S		N	A	G	S
L	U	A	U		L	I	F	T		B	E	R	E	T
E	M	E	R	G	E	S		S	A	Y				
		M	A	M	M	O	T	H	C	A	V	E		
D	O	N	U	T		O	R	A	T	O	R	I	O	
A	D	I	N		O	U	T	E	R		M	A	N	N
N	O	N	S	E	N	S	E		A	B	B	E	S	
G	R	A	N	D	T	E	T	O	N	S				
	A	D	O			R	E	S	T	A	T	E		
A	N	G	R	Y		G	E	N	S		I	L	I	A
C	O	A	L		G	R	E	A	T	F	A	L	L	S
I	S	L	E		S	I	L	T		E	R	O	D	E
D	Y	E	D		A	P	S	E		Y	A	W	E	D

ACTION NEEDED

History is simply a piece of paper covered with print; the main thing is still to make history, not to write it.
—Prince Otto von Bismarck

USING ONE'S NOODLE

Few people think more than two or three times a year. I have made an international reputation for myself by thinking once or twice a week.
—George Bernard Shaw

IT DOESN'T TAKE AN ARMY

Never doubt that a small group of thoughtful, committed citizens can change the world. Indeed, it is the only thing that ever has.
—Margaret Mead

TRIPLE PLAY

A good head and good heart are always a formidable combination. But when you add to that a literate tongue or pen, then you have something very special.
—Nelson Mandela

WOMEN OF COUNTRY MUSIC

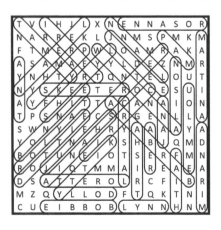

CAREGIVER QUALITIES

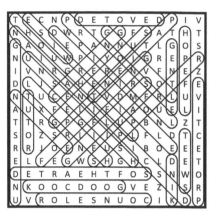

VALENTINE'S DAY

PLACES TO GO SKIING

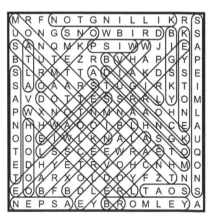

POPCORN

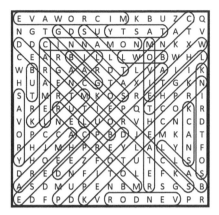

PORTMANTEAU WORDS

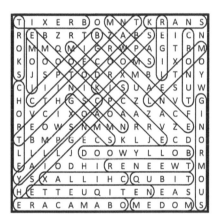

ROCK AND ROLL HALL OF FAME

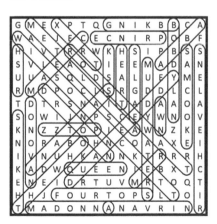

CALCUDOKU 2

¹1	¹²ˣ4	⁶ˣ2	3
¹²ˣ4	3	⁵⁺1	¹⁻2
3	²ː2	4	1
²2	1	¹⁻3	4

CALCUDOKU 3

³3	⁴ˣ4	1	³⁺2
²2	⁵⁺3	¹⁻4	1
⁴ˣ1	2	3	¹⁻4
4	¹⁻1	2	3

CALCUDOKU 4

¹⁻4	3	¹1	¹²⁺2	5
³⁺2	1	⁴4	5	⁶ˣ3
⁹⁺5	4	³ː3	1	2
⁴⁺3	¹²⁺5	²⁻2	4	⁸⁺1
1	2	5	3	4

CALCUDOKU 5

⁷⁺3	2	⁹⁺4	5	⁴ː1
2	⁶⁺5	²⁻1	⁵⁺3	4
⁸⁺4	1	3	2	⁵5
1	3	²⁻5	⁸ˣ4	2
²⁰ˣ5	4	2	1	³3

CALCUDOKU 6

⁸ˣ2	¹⁻4	3	⁵5	³ː1
4	⁴⁻1	5	²ː2	3
⁵ː5	¹⁰⁺3	2	1	²⁴ˣ4
1	5	²ː4	3	2
³3	2	1	⁹⁺4	5

CALCUDOKU 7

⁸⁺5	3	⁴4	⁵ː1	²ˣ2
⁴4	²⁻2	¹⁻3	5	1
⁵⁺1	4	2	⁶ˣ3	⁹⁺5
3	1	¹¹⁺5	2	4
²2	5	1	⁷⁺4	3

SUDOKU 2

3	7	5	8	1	4	2	6	9
8	6	9	2	3	5	1	7	4
2	4	1	7	6	9	5	8	3
9	5	8	4	7	6	3	1	2
4	1	6	3	8	2	9	5	7
7	3	2	9	5	1	8	4	6
5	2	3	1	4	7	6	9	8
6	9	4	5	2	8	7	3	1
1	8	7	6	9	3	4	2	5

SUDOKU 5

4	1	5	8	3	9	7	2	6
9	8	2	6	7	4	5	3	1
3	6	7	5	2	1	4	9	8
8	9	3	7	5	2	1	6	4
7	2	4	1	8	6	3	5	9
1	5	6	9	4	3	8	7	2
6	4	8	3	9	7	2	1	5
5	3	9	2	1	8	6	4	7
2	7	1	4	6	5	9	8	3

SUDOKU 3

5	6	8	3	2	7	1	9	4
3	7	2	9	4	1	5	8	6
1	9	4	8	6	5	7	3	2
2	4	5	7	3	8	6	1	9
7	8	9	4	1	6	2	5	3
6	3	1	5	9	2	8	4	7
8	2	3	1	7	9	4	6	5
4	5	7	6	8	3	9	2	1
9	1	6	2	5	4	3	7	8

SUDOKU 6

9	8	1	6	7	2	3	4	5
2	3	5	1	8	4	7	6	9
7	6	4	3	5	9	2	1	8
1	2	3	5	9	8	4	7	6
5	7	8	2	4	6	1	9	3
4	9	6	7	1	3	5	8	2
3	1	9	4	6	5	8	2	7
6	5	7	8	2	1	9	3	4
8	4	2	9	3	7	6	5	1

SUDOKU 4

5	1	9	8	4	2	6	7	3
4	6	2	7	9	3	8	1	5
3	8	7	6	5	1	9	2	4
7	4	8	5	6	9	1	3	2
6	2	5	3	1	4	7	9	8
1	9	3	2	7	8	5	4	6
8	7	1	4	2	5	3	6	9
9	3	4	1	8	6	2	5	7
2	5	6	9	3	7	4	8	1

SUDOKU 7

1	5	6	7	2	3	4	8	9
7	2	9	4	1	8	3	5	6
3	4	8	6	5	9	2	1	7
4	1	2	8	3	6	9	7	5
9	6	7	5	4	1	8	2	3
5	8	3	2	9	7	1	6	4
2	9	4	1	7	5	6	3	8
6	3	5	9	8	2	7	4	1
8	7	1	3	6	4	5	9	2

VACATION PLANS

Jackie, New England, visiting friends
Jane, South America, at a resort
Jim, Europe, guided tour
Joe, Southeast Asia, backpacking

SANDWICH PLATTERS

ham, ciabatta, potato salad
roast beef, sourdough, French fries
pastrami, whole wheat, coleslaw
turkey, pita bread, corn chips

MEETING SCHEDULE

Clara, traffic ticket, 2:00
Claude, incorporation, 3:00
Cletus, contract, 4:15
Cloris, will, 2:30

BARBECUE COOK-OFF

Beulah, Memphis, beef brisket
Billy Bob, Kansas City, baby
back ribs
Bryant, Texas, pulled pork
Buck, North Carolina, beef ribs

HOUSE HUNTING

Hal and Hallie, near schools,
30-year fixed
Ollie, big backyard, 5-year variable
Marian, extra bedroom,
15-year fixed
Ed and Ellie, swimming pool,
1-year variable

Medium Puzzles

WE'VE GOT YOUR NUMBER

P	A	S	S		O	W	E	N		A	M	M	A	N
A	C	M	E		R	O	M	E		L	I	A	N	A
P	I	O	N	E	E	R	E	D		C	A	D	D	Y
A	D	O		R	O	L	E			O	O	H		
W	I	C	C	A		D	R	I	F	T	W	O	O	D
S	C	H	U	S	S			O	U	T		U	R	N
			R	E	W	O	U	N	D		A	S	E	A
	H	I	D	D	E	N	F	I	G	U	R	E	S	
N	U	N	S		D	I	O	C	E	S	E			
O	L	D		S	E	C		S	A	N	D	A	L	
R	A	I	N	I	N	E	S	S		G	A	U	G	E
	G	U	M			Y	A	L	E			P	E	T
T	W	E	R	P		I	N	S	I	S	T	E	N	T
S	E	N	S	E		R	O	S	E		A	R	T	E
P	E	T	E	R		E	D	Y	S		U	S	S	R

TRIPLE PLAY

A	P	P		S	E	S	A	M	E		T	E	S	S
R	O	E		L	A	A	G	E	R		H	U	C	K
C	O	S	T	A	R	R	I	N	G		A	G	R	A
S	H	O	R	T		A	N	D		S	W	E	E	T
			U	S	E	S		S	I	T		N	E	E
O	M	A	N		N	O	R		R	A	V	E	N	S
P	A	N	C	E	T	T	A		E	V	E			
T	R	I	A	L		A	N	D		E	R	R	O	R
			T	E	E		B	R	I	S	B	A	N	E
T	H	I	E	V	E		Y	E	A		I	T	E	M
W	E	T		E	L	F		A	L	D	A			
A	G	A	I	N		A	N	D		A	G	A	I	N
N	I	L	S		P	R	E	F	E	R	E	N	C	E
G	R	I	M		A	S	S	U	R	E		T	O	W
S	A	C	S		T	I	T	L	E	S		I	N	S

LITERALLY SPEAKING

B	A	L	I		D	E	A	F		S	U	M	A	C
O	R	A	N		R	A	N	I		O	N	I	C	E
M	E	N	A	G	E	R	I	E		I	D	L	E	S
B	A	D	N	E	W	S		S	C	R	E	E	D	S
E	S	S	E	N					T	I	E	R		
			R	U	M	M	A	G	E	S	A	L	E	
T	E	S	S	E	R	A	E			S	O	L	A	R
E	R	I	N		L	O	L	L	S		L	O	I	N
A	D	L	I	B		B	O	A	R	D	E	R	S	
			E	N	I	D			N	A	M	E	S	
S	E	A	L	A	N	E		C	O	A	X	I	A	L
C	U	M	I	N		M	I	D	D	L	E	A	G	E
A	R	E	N	A		A	L	I	E		L	O	R	E
T	O	N	G	S		S	K	I	S		S	U	E	T

IN THE SWIM OF THINGS

A	B	E	A	M		D	A	T	A			P	G	A
P	O	S	S	E		A	J	A	R		C	H	I	C
B	A	C	K	S	T	R	O	K	E		P	E	R	T
S	T	A		N	O	T		E	N	F	O	L	D	S
			P	R	E	P		L	I	A	R		P	L	O
F	L	E	A		C	A	E	N		E	B	S	E	N
D	E	E	P	D	O	W	N			U	S	A		
A	U	S	T	R	A	L	I	A	N	C	R	A	W	L
			O	U	T		E	N	F	O	R	C	E	S
M	A	O	R	I		G	N	A	R		I	C	E	D
E	E	C		D	R	A	T		O	B	O	E		
D	R	E	S	S	E	R		A	C	E		D	I	E
L	A	L	A		S	N	O	R	K	E	L	I	N	G
E	T	O	N		T	E	R	M		R	O	N	D	O
Y	E	T		S	T	A	Y		Y	U	G	O	S	

GET YOUR BEARINGS

W	H	I	M		I	D	E	S	T		M	A	M	A
A	O	N	E		*N*	*O*	*R*	*T*	*H*		E	R	I	N
S	P	O	R	T	S	W	E	A	R		D	E	S	K
P	E	N	G	U	I	N		G	O	L	I	A	T	H
			E	L	D		*C*	*Y*	*N*	*I*	*C*			
S	A	N	D	I	E	G	*O*		G	R	A	Y	E	D
E	L	I		P	R	O	M	*O*		A	R	E	N	A
W	*E*	*S*	*T*		S	E	P	T	S		*E*	*A*	*S*	*T*
E	P	E	E	S		S	*A*	I	T	H		R	U	E
R	H	I	N	O	S		*S*	C	R	E	E	N	E	D
			T	A	L	*C*	*S*		A	N	D			
M	A	L	A	R	I	A		L	I	C	E	N	S	E
E	P	I	C		E	N	G	A	G	E	M	E	N	T
R	E	E	L		*S*	*O*	*U*	*T*	*H*		A	R	I	A
E	R	N	E		T	E	N	E	T		S	O	P	S

DROP-DOWN MENU

C	A	L	I	F		M	F	A	S		A	F	A	R
A	M	E	B	A		I	A	G	O		P	A	R	E
B	A	G	E	L		G	L	E	N		P	L	E	A
S	H	O	A	L	S		L	E	A	F		L	A	P
			M	I	N	E	O		T	A	T	A		
A	E	F		N	A	N	U		A	L	A	S	K	A
M	C	A		G	R	I	T			L	U	L	U	S
A	L	L	O	W	E	D		L	I	T	T	E	R	S
S	A	L	S	A		F	A	R	O		E	D	E	
S	T	I	L	T	S		A	T	O	P		P	S	T
			N	O	E	L		I	F	N	I	N		
G	E	L		R	I	L	L		Y	E	A	S	T	Y
A	D	O	S		P	A	G	E		C	O	P	R	A
L	I	V	E		O	N	U	S		E	M	A	I	L
S	T	E	W		N	A	Y	S		S	I	N	G	E

GOOD LOCATIONS

H	A	R	P		H	A	L	L	E		M	I	M	E
U	T	A	H		A	R	I	E	S		E	N	O	L
B	E	D	O	F	R	O	S	E	S		A	C	T	I
			T	U	T	U		E	A	G	L	E	S	
B	O	S	O	N		S	H	A	N	G	R	I	L	A
A	U	T	O		K	E	E	L		E	E	N		
S	T	A	P	L	E		C	O	R	N		A	B	A
E	R	G		I	N	S	T	E	A	D		T	O	T
L	E	I		C	O	L	A		T	A	P	I	R	S
			N	T	H		A	R	E	S		A	O	N	E
H	O	G	H	E	A	V	E	N		A	P	N	E	A
U	N	A	W	E	D		Z	A	N	Y				
L	I	R	A		E	A	S	Y	S	T	R	E	E	T
A	C	E	R		P	L	U	M	E		U	N	T	O
S	E	A	T		T	I	N	E	S		S	E	A	M

OFF-SEASON BLUES

People ask me what I do in the winter when there's no baseball. I'll tell you what I do. I stare out the window and wait for spring.
—Rogers Hornsby

WHAT COMES FIRST

Courage is the most important of all the virtues because without courage, you can't practice any other virtue consistently.
—Maya Angelou

WHEN THINGS CLICK

The meeting of two personalities is like the contact of two chemical substances: if there is any reaction, both are transformed.
—Carl Gustav Jung

THINK ABOUT THE INSCRUTABLE

The most beautiful experience we can have is the mysterious. It is the fundamental emotion that stands at the cradle of true art and true science.
—Albert Einstein

RIMSHOT, PLEASE

I came from a real tough neighborhood. Once a guy pulled a knife on me. I knew he wasn't a professional, the knife had butter on it.
—Rodney Dangerfield

NO LAUGHING MATTER

Humor is a serious thing. I like to think of it as one of our greatest earliest natural resources, which must be preserved at all costs.
—James Thurber

SHOW ME THE MONEY!

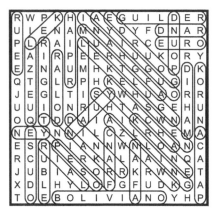

FAMOUS GOLFERS

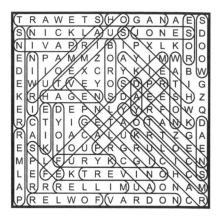

SUMMER OLYMPICS

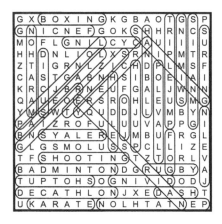

POPULAR STREET NAMES

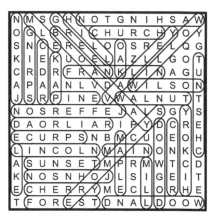

VEGGIES

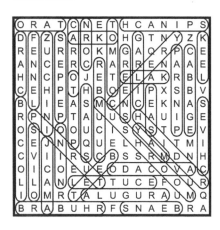

LET ME "RE" WORD THAT

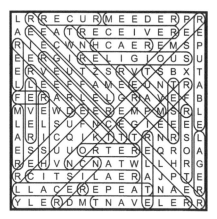

CALCUDOKU 8

15+ 5	6	4 4	5+ 2	3	4+ 1
6 6	4	1 1	12+ 5	2	3
3+ 1	4+ 3	7+ 2	7+ 4	5	6 6
2	1	5	3	10+ 6	4
4 4	5 5	3 3	8+ 6	1	7+ 2
5+ 3	2	6 6	1	4 4	5

CALCUDOKU 11

3- 6	7+ 2	1 1	1- 4	5	3 3
3	5	3: 2	24x 6	4	10x 1
4 4	3- 3	6	0- 1	2	5
4- 5	6	3 3	2	1	2: 4
1	4 4	5 5	12+ 3	18x 6	2
2: 2	1	4	5	3	6 6

CALCUDOKU 9

5 5	11+ 6	1 1	7+ 4	3	2 2
6+ 1	5	6 6	8+ 3	6+ 2	4
3	2	6+ 4	5	10+ 1	6 6
9+ 6	3	2	3+ 1	4	5
5+ 4	1	8+ 5	2	6 6	9+ 3
2 2	4 4	3	6 6	5	1

CALCUDOKU 12

6x 2	3	1- 4	5	0- 6	1
6 6	4 4	2 2	3 3	4x 1	5
10x 5	2	5- 6	1	4	2: 3
20x 1	5	15x 3	4 4	6x 2	6
4	1 1	5	4- 6	3	40x 2
2: 3	6	1 1	2	5	4

CALCUDOKU 10

2 2	4 4	9+ 6	3	7+ 5	1 1
11+ 5	4+ 1	3	8+ 6	2	9+ 4
6	7+ 3	4	2	1 1	5
1 1	7+ 5	2	9+ 4	15+ 6	3
13+ 3	2 2	7+ 1	5	4	6
4	6	5	1	5+ 3	2

CALCUDOKU 13

0- 1	2	2- 4	2- 6	5 5	15x 3
3	2- 6	2	4	1 1	5
1- 5	4	1 1	2 2	3 3	10+ 6
6	2- 5	3	6x 1	2	4
5+ 4	1	30x 5	3	6 6	2 2
6x 2	3	6	9+ 5	4	1 1

SUDOKU 8

6	1	9	7	3	8	5	4	2
2	3	4	5	1	6	8	9	7
8	5	7	9	4	2	6	3	1
9	8	2	1	6	3	7	5	4
5	7	6	4	2	9	3	1	8
1	4	3	8	5	7	9	2	6
7	2	5	3	8	1	4	6	9
4	9	1	6	7	5	2	8	3
3	6	8	2	9	4	1	7	5

SUDOKU 9

2	7	6	3	8	9	4	5	1
5	1	8	7	6	4	3	2	9
4	9	3	2	1	5	8	7	6
1	6	7	8	9	3	2	4	5
3	5	9	4	2	6	1	8	7
8	2	4	5	7	1	9	6	3
7	8	1	9	5	2	6	3	4
6	3	5	1	4	8	7	9	2
9	4	2	6	3	7	5	1	8

SUDOKU 10

9	3	2	6	1	4	8	7	5
4	6	7	5	9	8	3	1	2
5	8	1	7	3	2	6	9	4
8	1	3	4	7	6	2	5	9
2	4	6	8	5	9	7	3	1
7	5	9	1	2	3	4	8	6
6	9	5	3	4	7	1	2	8
1	7	8	2	6	5	9	4	3
3	2	4	9	8	1	5	6	7

SUDOKU 11

2	6	5	1	9	3	8	7	4
4	9	3	7	8	2	6	5	1
7	1	8	4	5	6	2	3	9
6	8	7	9	3	4	1	2	5
9	3	1	2	6	5	7	4	8
5	2	4	8	1	7	9	6	3
1	4	6	5	2	9	3	8	7
3	7	9	6	4	8	5	1	2
8	5	2	3	7	1	4	9	6

SUDOKU 12

3	1	6	4	2	8	9	5	7
4	5	2	3	9	7	1	6	8
7	8	9	5	6	1	3	4	2
8	6	4	7	3	9	2	1	5
5	7	1	6	4	2	8	3	9
2	9	3	8	1	5	6	7	4
1	3	8	9	7	4	5	2	6
6	4	5	2	8	3	7	9	1
9	2	7	1	5	6	4	8	3

SUDOKU 13

9	7	6	1	2	8	3	5	4
2	3	4	9	5	7	8	1	6
8	5	1	4	6	3	7	9	2
5	8	7	6	4	1	9	2	3
4	9	2	3	8	5	1	6	7
6	1	3	7	9	2	4	8	5
3	2	8	5	1	4	6	7	9
7	6	5	8	3	9	2	4	1
1	4	9	2	7	6	5	3	8

GOLF TOURNAMENT

Gary, best with irons, titanium shafts, 72

Gordon, chipping champ, hybrid clubs, 75

Grant, long driver, oversized putter, 71

Greg, tops in putting, 60° wedge, 69

BACKYARD GARDEN PLANS

Pam Peatmoss, hydrangeas, cucumbers, 140 sq. ft.

Pat Planter, daylilies, tomatoes, 100 sq. ft.

Penny Pruner, begonias, squash, 150 sq. ft.

Portia Pullweeds, marigolds, eggplant, 125 sq. ft.

A DAY AT THE BEACH

Samantha, sodas, playing cards, novel

Sandi, ice cream treats, beach ball, magazine

Skip, chips, Frisbee, puzzle book

Stu, cookies, badminton set, newspaper

STOCKING THE SHELVES

Carrots, Quick Veggies, 24 oz, 5

Green beans, Super Fresh, 12 oz, 7

Peas, Happy Eats, 8 oz, 15

Sweet corn, store brand, 16 oz, 10

EASTER BASKETS

Erin Jones, pink, 10, gummies

Tommy Jones, green, 7, marshmallows

Emma Baker, yellow, 8, jelly beans

Brian Baker, blue, 12, candy corn

PUTTING IN THE CROPS

Sam, 120 acres, wheat, forward contract

Sandra, 60 acres, soybeans, drip irrigation

Scott, 40 acres, rice, crop-dusting

Sean, 80 acres, corn, biotech seeds

BASEBALL FRONT OFFICE ANALYSIS

Don Dinger, $6 million, 32, 309

Harry Hitter, $10 million, 37, 332

Sal Smasher, $7.3 million, 41, 280

Sid Slugger, $8.5 million, 50, 315

Difficult Puzzles

HIGH GRADE

C	O	O	L		S	P	A	M		S	M	O	T	E
A	L	M	A		I	R	M	A		T	A	T	E	R
F	A	I	R	T	R	E	E	S		E	S	T	E	R
E	S	T	E	E		A	N	A		A	T	O	M	S
			D	E	R	M		L	A	L	O			
N	O	T	O	N	A	B	E	A	T		D	O	W	D
E	R	A		I	T	L	L		S	O	O	T	H	E
P	A	S	T	E		E	O	N		U	N	T	I	L
A	T	T	I	R	E		P	E	L	T		E	S	T
L	E	E	R		T	H	E	M	E	P	A	R	K	A
			A	L	S	O		A	A	A	S			
E	D	E	M	A		B	A	T		C	I	R	C	A
T	R	A	I	N		A	T	O	N	E	D	E	A	F
N	O	R	S	E		R	O	D	E		E	A	S	E
A	P	L	U	S		T	I	E	D		S	P	E	W

RIVALRIES

A	T	T	A		B	A	R	E	S		M	I	R	A
G	I	R	D		A	S	S	A	I		A	D	E	N
R	A	I	D	E	R	S	V	S	C	H	I	E	F	S
E	R	E		U	N	A	P	T		O	N	O		
E	A	R	D	R	U	M		C	O	W	S	L	I	P
			R	E	M		L	O	L	L		O	N	E
B	A	T	I	K		H	E	A	L		O	G	E	E
A	L	A	B	A	M	A	V	S	A	U	B	U	R	N
I	B	I	S		O	N	I	T		P	O	E	T	S
R	E	L		D	O	G	S		A	R	E			
N	E	W	L	I	N	E		F	L	O	S	S	E	S
		I	A	N		R	O	O	F	S		A	B	A
Y	A	N	K	E	E	S	V	S	R	E	D	S	O	X
O	L	D	E		N	O	I	S	E		O	S	L	O
M	E	S	S		E	N	D	E	D		D	Y	A	N

EASY AS ABC

T	A	B	O	O		P	O	N	G		W	O	K	S
S	N	O	O	K		A	R	A	L		A	C	N	E
A	N	T	H	R	O	P	O	M	O	R	P	H	I	C
R	U	T		A	V	E		E	G	O	I	S	T	S
S	L	O	P		A	R	P		G	M	T			
		M	A	D		S	H	E		A	I	S	L	E
I	M	M	U	R	E		O	V	E	N		A	U	K
B	I	O	L	U	M	I	N	E	S	C	E	N	C	E
I	N	S		I	S	L	E		T	E	N	D	E	D
S	I	T	E	D		K	I	N		S	O	W		
			G	I	N		N	E	E		L	I	S	P
O	V	E	R	S	E	E		I	R	K		C	I	A
C	I	N	E	M	A	T	O	G	R	A	P	H	E	R
T	A	C	T		R	U	S	H		L	I	E	G	E
O	L	E	S		S	I	T	S		E	N	D	E	D

DIMENSIONS

B	A	A	L		S	P	O	T		F	O	S	S	E
A	L	T	A		V	I	N	E		L	I	M	E	D
L	I	T	T	L	E	T	O	E		E	L	A	T	E
T	S	A	R	I	N	A		M	I	X		L	A	N
S	T	R	O	N	G		R	I	L	L				
			B	E	A	R		R	E	B	A	T	E	S
B	A	B	E		L	A	M	E		L	O	I	R	E
A	N	I		S	I	Z	A	B	L	E		M	I	N
B	O	G	I	E		E	P	E	E		D	E	E	D
U	N	L	O	A	D	S		L	A	K	E			
			E	N	O	S		K	A	F	T	A	N	
A	G	A		T	L	C		P	A	L	E	R	M	O
I	N	G	O	T		L	A	R	G	E	C	A	P	S
M	A	U	V	E		O	B	O	E		T	I	L	E
S	W	E	A	R		G	A	P	S		S	L	E	D

HINT, HINT

A	R	E	A		E	T	A	L		M	A	M	A	S
B	A	R	N		R	U	S	E		E	M	O	T	E
S	P	R	I	N	G	B	O	K		S	N	O	O	T
			M	U	S	I	C		P	A	E	L	L	A
A	L	L	I	N		N	I	L	E		S	A	L	T
A	L	A	S		A	G	A	I	N	S	T			
R	A	P	T	O	R		L	E	A	P	Y	E	A	R
G	N	U		L	E	U		D	N	A		A	L	E
H	O	P	A	L	O	N	G		C	R	I	T	I	C
			G	A	L	I	L	E	E		N	E	S	T
S	L	O	E		A	X	O	N		L	E	N	T	O
T	I	L	L	E	R		B	A	S	E	R			
A	L	D	E	R		J	U	M	P	S	T	A	R	T
B	L	E	S	S		A	L	O	E		I	R	I	S
S	E	N	S	E		N	E	R	D		A	T	O	P

BIG BLUE MARBLE

L	A	M	A		B	O	T	T	O	M		T	I	C
U	F	O	S		E	R	R	A	T	A		R	O	E
M	O	T	H	E	R	E	A	R	T	H		E	N	D
P	U	T		A	T	O	P		L	E	A	S	E	
S	L	O	U	G	H		S	T	E	P	S			
			P	L	A	N	E	T	A	R	I	U	M	S
T	H	E	S	E		O	R	Y	X		C	R	E	E
H	U	N		S	O	M	A	L	I	A		E	N	G
U	L	N	A		R	O	T	E		V	I	R	E	O
G	L	O	B	E	T	R	O	T	T	E	R			
			B	L	A	S	E		E	N	R	A	G	E
F	I	L	E	R		B	E	R	G		D	O	N	
A	L	I		W	O	R	L	D	S	E	R	I	E	S
S	I	N		I	C	E	A	G	E		P	E	R	U
T	A	G		G	A	T	H	E	R		M	U	S	E

WHAT'S IN A NAME?

E	L	S	E		C	O	M	A		A	B	E	A	M
D	O	C	S		O	R	E	S		D	R	A	C	O
W	A	R	P		A	C	A	I		M	A	C	R	O
A	F	A	R		S	A	N	D	W	I	C	H	E	S
R	E	P	E	A	T		D	E	E	R	E			
D	R	E	S	S	E	S		R	A	S	H	L	Y	
			S	H	R	A	P	N	E	L		A	Y	E
H	E	R	O		A	H	A		I	D	E	S		
I	R	A		C	A	R	D	I	G	A	N			
S	A	F	A	R	I		R	A	G	T	I	M	E	
		G	E	N	T	S		T	O	E	C	A	P	
S	I	L	H	O	U	E	T	T	E		R	E	N	O
I	D	E	A	L		A	R	O	W		N	A	A	N
D	E	N	S	E		M	E	G	A		E	G	G	Y
E	A	S	T	S		S	W	A	Y		T	E	E	M

MOVE ON

Finish each day and be done with it. You have done what you could. Some blunders and absurdities no doubt crept in; forget them as soon as you can. Tomorrow is a new day. You shall begin it serenely and with too high a spirit to be encumbered with your old nonsense.
—Ralph Waldo Emerson

TO SUM THINGS UP

If you had to identify in one word the reason why the human race has not achieved and never will achieve its full potential, that word would be "meetings."
—Dave Barry

LIGHTEN UP

We should consider every day lost on which we have not danced at least once. And we should call every truth false which was not accompanied by at least one laugh.
—Friedrich Nietzsche

DEEP THOUGHT

Beauty is an experience, nothing else. It is not a fixed pattern or an arrangement of features. It is something felt, a glow or a communicated sensed fineness.
—D.H. Lawrence

A COMMON TRAIT

Faced with the choice between changing one's mind and proving that there is no need to do so, almost everyone gets busy on the proof.
—John Kenneth Galbraith

KEEP TRYING NEW THINGS

After all these years, I am still involved in the process of self-discovery. It's better to explore life and make mistakes than to play it safe. Mistakes are part of the dues one pays for a full life.
—Sophia Loren

DOG BREEDS

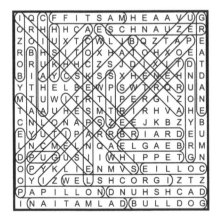

PRECIOUS STONES

CALIFORNIA TOWNS NAMED AFTER SPANISH SAINTS

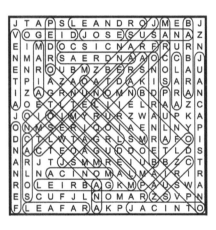

INTERNATIONAL TRAVEL

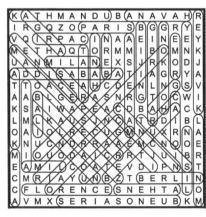

ANIMAL GROUP NAMES

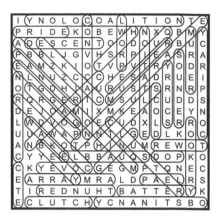

US MOUNTAIN PEAKS

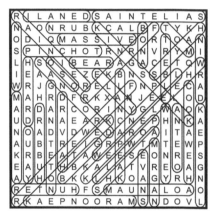

TYPES OF PASTA

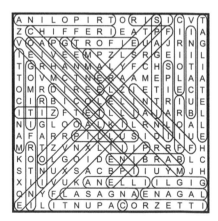

CALCUDOKU 14

1-6	1	3:3	4-2	100×4	5
4	2:3	1	6	5	1-2
3+1	6	14+4	5	2	3
2	15+4	5	3	2-1	24×6
15×5	9+2	6	11+1	3	4
3	5	2	4	6	1·1

CALCUDOKU 17

6×6	1	2-5	13+2	12+3	4
4×1	10×2	3	6	4	5
4	5	8×2	1	1:6	3
5+3	1-6	4	2-5	2	1
2	4	1	3	5:5	3:6
90×5	3	6	4·4	1	2

SUDOKU 14

8	4	3	9	2	5	1	7	6
2	9	1	7	3	6	4	5	8
7	6	5	8	1	4	2	3	9
3	8	2	4	5	1	9	6	7
4	5	7	6	9	8	3	2	1
9	1	6	3	7	2	5	8	4
5	3	8	1	6	9	7	4	2
6	2	9	5	4	7	8	1	3
1	7	4	2	8	3	6	9	5

CALCUDOKU 15

2:4	3-3	6	6+5	1	2·2
2	2×1	14+5	6	13+3	4
5:5	2	1	3	1-4	6
1	16+6	4	1-2	5	2-3
90×3	4	2	1	13+6	5
6	5	3·3	4	2	1

CALCUDOKU 18

30×5	2-1	6	40×4	1-3	2
6	3	4:4	5	2	6+1
2:2	4	1	72×3	6·6	5
1	7+5	3	2	4	9+6
144×4	2	30×5	6	5:1	3
3	6	2	1·1	5	4·4

SUDOKU 15

7	9	1	5	3	6	4	2	8
8	3	2	4	1	9	7	6	5
5	4	6	2	7	8	1	3	9
2	7	8	3	6	4	5	9	1
4	6	3	9	5	1	2	8	7
9	1	5	7	8	2	6	4	3
3	8	7	6	4	5	9	1	2
6	5	9	1	2	3	8	7	4
1	2	4	8	9	7	3	5	6

CALCUDOKU 16

2:3	6	1-4	3-1	5	4-2
7+2	5·5	3	1-4	1	6
1	4	1-6	5	8×2	3·3
17+6	3·3	5	3:2	4	1
5	2	2×1	6	270×3·4	4
4	1·1	2	3	6	5

CALCUDOKU 19

72×6	6+4	2	0-1	3	6+5
4	3	30×5	6	2	1
10×2	1	6	12+5	12×4	3
5	3-2	4	3	36×1	6
2-1	5	6×3	2	6	8×4
3	5-6	1	20×4	5	2

SUDOKU 16

1	7	2	3	4	9	5	6	8
9	6	5	8	2	1	7	4	3
8	3	4	7	6	5	9	2	1
2	1	7	6	3	8	4	5	9
6	9	3	5	1	4	2	8	7
4	5	8	2	9	7	3	1	6
3	4	6	1	7	2	8	9	5
5	2	1	9	8	3	6	7	4
7	8	9	4	5	6	1	3	2

SUDOKU 17

6	1	7	3	2	8	9	4	5
2	3	4	9	1	5	7	8	6
9	8	5	7	4	6	1	3	2
3	5	2	4	9	1	6	7	8
8	4	9	6	5	7	2	1	3
7	6	1	2	8	3	5	9	4
4	7	3	5	6	9	8	2	1
5	9	8	1	3	2	4	6	7
1	2	6	8	7	4	3	5	9

SUDOKU 18

6	7	2	1	3	4	5	9	8
4	1	5	7	8	9	6	2	3
8	9	3	6	2	5	7	1	4
1	6	4	5	7	2	8	3	9
2	3	9	8	4	6	1	7	5
7	5	8	9	1	3	2	4	6
3	8	7	4	5	1	9	6	2
5	2	6	3	9	7	4	8	1
9	4	1	2	6	8	3	5	7

SUDOKU 19

9	1	5	2	8	6	4	7	3
7	4	2	1	3	9	8	5	6
3	6	8	5	7	4	9	1	2
1	7	9	3	2	5	6	4	8
8	3	6	7	4	1	5	2	9
2	5	4	9	6	8	1	3	7
6	2	1	4	9	7	3	8	5
4	8	3	6	5	2	7	9	1
5	9	7	8	1	3	2	6	4

FRIDAY NIGHT POKER GAME

Pam, Texas Hold'em, corn chips, + **$5.**75

Paul, deuces wild, peanuts, - **$8.**40

Penny, stud poker, pretzels, - **$7.**50

Perry, high-low split, potato chips, broke even

Phil, draw poker, popcorn, + **$10.**15

BOND PORTFOLIO

Great Ventures, A-1, 7 years, $2,500,000

Jones & Smith, C, 12 years, $3,000,000

Prime Products, B-1, 5 years, $1,000,000

SudoCo, A-2, 10 years, $1,250,000

United Businesses, B-2, 15 years, $1,500,000

FAVORITE NEWS FEEDS

Nate, CNB, sport stories, puzzles

Ned, NewsHost, instant news alerts, sport scores

Nora, eJournal, entertainment news, human-interest stories

Nell, NY Sentinel, in-depth analyses, business updates

Nils, AggreGator, strong reporting staff, political reports

BIRTHDAY LUNCH

Cristy, moo shu beef, egg drop, spring roll

Carla, Szechuan pork, hot and sour soup, steamed dumplings

Kate, vegetable lo mein, seafood, edamame

Kayla, kung pao chicken, pork noodle, fried wonton

Kiki, Gen. Tso's shrimp, vegetable, barbecued ribs

OFFICE SUPPLY STORE RUN

Sam, laptop case, binder clips, blue felt-tip pens

Seth, keyboard/mouse, ruler, 0.7 mm mech. pencil

Sid, replacement chair, 3x5 cards, black ballpoint pens

Stan, printer cartridge, paper clips, red felt-tip pens

Tiffany, reading lamp, sticky notes, mech. pencil lead

HIGH SCHOOL SPORTS PROGRAMS

Mr. Adams, Rugby, 24, $7,200

Mr. Baker, Golf, 20, $6,000

Ms. Cartwright, Field hockey, 35, $5,000

Ms. Davis, Rowing, 30, $7,500

Mr. Edison, Swimming, 25, $6,500

ACKNOWLEDGMENTS

I deeply appreciate the important contribution Patrick Min made to this book—he constructed all the delightful calcudoku puzzles that are included in it. Patrick is an accomplished puzzle master and oversees the premier calcudoku website, calcudoku.org. I heartily recommend you pay a visit to the site for more calcudoku-solving fun.

ABOUT THE AUTHOR

Phil Fraas is a longtime constructor of crossword puzzles. He started in the early 1980s when he had several of his first efforts published in the *New York Times*. He now oversees and constructs puzzles for a free crossword, sudoku, and word search puzzle website—YourPuzzleSource.com.